D1481033

The President's House Is Empty

This issue of *Forum* is made possible by the generous support of the William and Flora Hewlett Foundation, Incite Labs, the National Endowment for the Arts, and an anonymous donor.

Editors-in-Chief Deborah Chasman, Joshua Cohen

Managing Editor Adam McGee

Senior Editor Chloe Fox

Web and Production Editor Avni Majithia-Sejpal

Poetry Editors Timothy Donnelly, BK Fischer, Stefania Heim

Fiction Editor Junot Díaz

Editorial Assistants Lisa Borst, Will Holub-Moorman, Rachel Kennedy

Poetry Readers William Brewer, Julie Kantor, Becca Liu, Nick Narbutas, Diana Khoi Nguyen, Eleanor Sarasohn, Sean Zhuraw

Publisher Louisa Daniels Kearney

Marketing Manager Anne Boylan

Outreach Director Kira Brunner Don

Marketing Associate Michelle Betters

Finance Manager Anthony DeMusis III

Marketing Assistant Sara Barber

Magazine Distributor Disticor Magazine Distribution Services
800-668-7724, info@disticor.com

Book Orders Ingram Content Group
800-937-8000, customerservice@ingramcontent.com

Printer Quad Graphics

Board of Advisors Swati Mylavarapu & Derek Schrier (co-chairs), Archon Fung, Deborah Fung, Richard M. Locke, Jeff Mayersohn, Jennifer Moses, Scott Nielsen, Martha C. Nussbaum, Robert Pollin, Rob Reich, Hiram Samel, Kim Malone Scott

Graphic Design Zak Jensen

Typefaces Druk and Adobe Pro Caslon

To become a member or subscribe, visit:
bostonreview.net/membership/

For questions about book sales or publicity, contact:
Michelle Betters, michelle@bostonreview.net

For questions about subscriptions, call 877-406-2443
or email custsvc_bostonrv@fulcoinc.com.

Boston Review
PO Box 425786, Cambridge, MA 02142
617-324-1360

ISSN: 0734-2306

Authors retain copyright of their own work.
© 2017, Boston Critic, Inc.

Editors' Note

Deborah Chasman & Joshua Cohen

ON INAUGURATION DAY 2017, we published an essay by Bonnie Honig called "The President's House Is Empty." The online reaction was extraordinary—the piece went viral, sending a record number of readers to *Boston Review*'s website.

Honig's starting point—as in the updated version we are publishing here—was the President's announcement, made months earlier, that Melania and Barron Trump would not be moving into the White House. For Honig, this decision to "opt out" symbolically crystallized our increasing abandonment of public things—from education to clean water—and our diminishing sense of being a public who are "in it together" and who all depend on those things.

So when we brainstormed in early spring about urgent topics for this issue, and thought about environment, health care, and education, we were struck by the thread that tied them together: they could all be grouped under the idea of public goods—things that are arguably necessary for a decent life, that are owed to citizens of a democracy, and that provide a common space that we all share. In the United States today, these goods are endangered and access to them is constricted by class and race.

In this issue we consider these public goods: what they are, how to provide them, and how to ensure equitable access, whether they are delivered through the private or public sectors. More than that, several contributors suggest that the very act of defining and providing these public goods is constitutive: they help to give us a sense that we are a public, not simply a collection of individuals who live in the same place. As Sabeel Rahman writes in the lead essay to our forum, what is at stake is not only what we owe to each other, but who we are. If Rahman is right, then debate about public goods is at the same time debate about what it means to be an American.

We hope you are provoked by what you read here—and provoked enough to share and argue about it with your friends, neighbors, and colleagues. After all, the greatest public good in a democracy is democracy itself.

Chasman & Cohen

The President's House Is Empty

Bonnie Honig

IN NOVEMBER 2016 Donald Trump announced that his family would not live in the White House after the inauguration. His wife and son preferred to live in New York. Perhaps due to mounting public pressure—even from conservative Trump supporters, concerned with the optics of this unconventional First Family—or perhaps simply because the school year ended, Melania and Barron moved to the White House on June 12. The cost in security alone of having maintained a household for them in New York City is estimated to be about $24 million. Meanwhile, since taking office, Trump has made 24 trips to golf on his own courses, at a cost of about $3 million per trip. Many of these trips have been to his Florida resort, Mar-a-Lago—his so-called "winter White House"—where (as of mid-June) he has spent approximately 30 days of his presidency.

These choices have implications for all of us. Who will pay for all of the additional security necessitated by the decisions to maintain a second household and to frequent Trump resorts? Who has already borne the costs of the disruptions caused by repeated presidential flights to New York and Florida airports, not to mention motorcades in and out of midtown Manhattan and Palm Springs?

The answer, of course, has turned out to be: taxpayers—or, as we used to be called, the public. Many of those costs, racked up on Trump properties, will be paid right into the president's own pockets. For example, according to the *New York Post*, in addition to "the cost of agents, staff and equipment and barriers that are normal in such cases," security services protecting Trump's family in New York were obliged to *rent space* in Trump Tower at a cost of more than $3 million a year, to be paid to the president's own corporation. Secret Service agents protecting Trump in Florida have been billed for their use of golf carts to follow him on his rounds. Although *Politico* reported that Trump footed the bill for Japanese prime minister Shinzō Abe's stay at Mar-a-Lago, it was also reported that Trump promised to donate all money spent by foreign governments at his hotels to the Treasury so that he would not violate the Constitution's Emoluments Clause. But so far there is no sign that those donations have been made. On May 16 congressional Democrats introduced legislation that would order Trump to reimburse the federal government for any public money spent on trips to his private resorts. The bill is unlikely to go anywhere, however, and in the meantime the bipartisan congressional budget of early May guarantees that the federal government will pay New York for costs incurred protecting Melania's household.

This is galling because taxpayers already pay for a secure home and office for the president of the United States and his family. It is called the White House. The White House is a public thing to be used by the president and his or her family while in public office. The White House has an infrastructure of security that provides presidents and their families with the protection they need. What Trump and his family did was opt out of that public thing. They chose to go private. And in so doing, they incurred costs that they then passed on to the public. Their "free choice" was subsidized, as are so many "free" choices (charter schools, gated neighborhoods), by the public.

A president who lives at his private home(s) requires a mobile security apparatus and governance infrastructure. The public thing, the White House, enables certain efficiencies in the provision of security and administrative support but these are lost when the private option is preferred. The American public even provides the president with a holiday home, Camp David, which, because of its long use by presidents, also has in place the necessary infrastructure. However, Trump has spurned this home as well: "Have you seen it?" he said of Camp David, as if that were enough to explain his preference for his own commercial hotel and golf course, Mar-a-Lago. It seems obvious that, if a president disdains the homes the public provides for him, and thus foregoes their efficiencies, the resulting costs should be borne by him, the one who has opted out, and not by the very public whose public thing has been spurned. That is, Trump's family members are free to not use the residence provided by the public, but they should then be personally responsible for assuming the costs of that choice. They should not pass them on to us.

Beyond the monetary costs of the Trump opt-out, there are symbolic costs, as well. Here there may even be a lesson for Trump. Not that anyone expects him to learn it. Faced with the refusal of Mexico to pay for the much-promised border wall, Trump has said he expects U.S. taxpayers to pay for it (promising vaguely that Mexico will pay us back). But taxpayers have lost the habit of happily paying for public things and Trump, the one opting out, is in no position to revivify the habit. After years of neoliberalization, there is no reservoir of love for public things on which to draw, no exemplary public sacrifice to inspire. Recall when Khizr Khan, the Gold Star father, asked if Trump had ever sacrificed anything for his country. Trump's answer—given to a man whose son died fighting in Iraq—was that yes, he had sacrificed: to build a business.

Neoliberalism means many things to many people, but the one trait by which it is always distinguished is its approval of the opt-out and a willingness to turn a blind eye to the hidden costs of such a choice. Everything is optional for the neoliberal; this is how neoliberalism defines freedom. Neoliberals opt out of any collective thing they can afford to opt out of. They believe everyone should be free to send their children to private or charter schools, to live in private gated communities, to hire private transport rather than take the school bus, and so on. "Choice" is their watchword and choice is synonymous with freedom.

The hidden costs of opting out are not their problem. But they are ours. If the well-to-do do not use the public school system, the community is deprived of their energies and contributions. If they do not use city roads and sewage, they come to resent having to pay for the upkeep of infrastructure that others rely on. If fewer and fewer children take the school bus, it soon becomes an added expense to the public purse that cannot be justified, and suddenly there is no bus service, even if some need it—or else only its users are asked to pay for it, which raises costs and singles some people out. It should come as no surprise then that in recent debates about repealing the Affordable Care Act, some congressmen have asked why the healthy should "subsidize" the sick, thus betraying little understanding of the workings of insurance (in which those who are now healthy pay to indemnify themselves against the contingency of one day becoming sick) and of the very idea of democracy (in which redistributions are made to underwrite social equilibria that benefit everyone).

But there is a still worse cost. The democratic experiment involves living cheek by jowl with others, sharing classrooms, roads, and buses, paying for them together, complaining about them together, and sometimes even praising and enjoying them together, as picnickers will do on a sunny afternoon in Central Park. But the neoliberal corrective absolves us of this necessity and responsibility. One of the many sad ironies here is that Central Park—landscape architecture's ode to the power of democratic beauty—is just a stone's throw away from where barricades encircled Trump Tower from January to June.

All too often opting out depends on the public purse it pretends to circumvent. Charter schools and voucher programs invite locals to opt out of public schools while drawing on public funds that might have improved the public education system rather than provide an alternative to it. Someone is making money on charter schools and vouchers and it is not the community. Also, and more importantly—as Senator Maggie Hassan pointed out to Betsy DeVos at her confirmation hearing to become secretary of education—charter schools and voucher programs are not governed by public education's mandate to educate *all* students. Like the Affordable Care Act, which mandates providing health care coverage to those with preexisting conditions, a properly democratic education system mandates providing education to those with preexisting conditions, too, such as poverty, recent immigration, physical and learning disabilities, as well as other challenges that may make learning difficult. This democratic mandate to educate everyone is what charters and voucher systems opt out of. Such mandates are the last, dying breath of the public thing.

Why review the vexations of the neoliberal opt-out now? Because we will all feel the impact—both financial and symbolic—of the latest and most public one. Regardless of whether the White House is occupied by members of the First Family, their cavalier attitude toward it is a stark reminder of the emptiness of this presidency and its disdain for public things.

Honig

Losing and Gaining Public Goods

K. Sabeel Rahman

AS THE REPUBLICAN REPEAL of President Barack Obama's signature health care reform barreled forward this spring, leading conservatives framed their agenda in familiar terms. Mick Mulvaney, former Tea Party congressman and President Donald Trump's new budget director, asked why responsible taxpayers should "be required to take care of the person who sits home, drinks sugary drinks . . . and doesn't exercise, and eats poorly and gets diabetes."

Representative Jason Chaffetz (R-Utah) expressed the same finger-wagging sensibility with greater color: "Americans have choices. . . . So maybe, rather than getting that new iPhone that they just love and they want to go spend hundreds of dollars on, maybe they should invest that in health care."

Obamacare was the most significant expansion of the safety net since the War on Poverty—if not the New Deal—but for over seven years, conservatives alleged that this expansion led to governmental tyranny, unnecessary expense, and a decline in personal responsibility.

Yet to the surprise of many, the proposed replacement, which included brazen attempts to gut Medicaid and dismantle subsidies and nondiscrimination provisions, set off a firestorm of resistance from ordinary Americans. Protesters jammed lawmakers' offices, town halls, and phone lines. In crowds dwarfing the 2010 Tea Party protests against the Affordable Care Act, Americans voiced their opposition to the House repeal bill. These protests by and large called for the exact opposite of Mulvaney's critique: an *expansion* of health care as a "human right." In California statutes that would create a single-payer health care system are even now making their way through the legislature.

The protests were remarkable. But equally striking was the shift in the terms of public debate. The focus was no longer simply on the details of policy design. As one Texas protester put it, "The Republican health care bill is immoral. . . . It's wrong. I think health care is a right, not a privilege. And I do really think people are going to die." The protests raised fundamental issues of political morality: what do we owe each other as free and equal members of a democratic society?

The clash over health care is the most glaring example of a more widespread battle over the meaning and importance of public goods: what they are, how they ought to be provided—and to whom. The question of whether to privatize and deregulate, or to restore—and even expand—public provision is at the heart of many contemporary political, economic, and moral debates. At the federal level, the question over public provision manifests in disputes over privatizing education or slashing funds for affordable housing. On a more local level, the poisonous water of Flint, Michigan, exemplifies the toll of the larger trend of budget-cutting and privatizing vital public services.

Rahman

In economic terms, public goods are defined as being nonrivalrous and nonexcludable—meaning that one person's consumption does not preclude another's, and that it is difficult (or impossible) to prevent people from consuming the good without paying for it. Classic examples are light and air. A second, more conventional understanding of public goods focuses on the economics of production. Goods that have high sunk costs and increasing returns to scale are likely to be underprovided by ordinary market competition. Think cable TV and landlines: the massive expense involved in laying down wiring on a national scale discourages private investment, but the benefits of a national network increase as the network grows. These conventional public goods are therefore seen as a proper domain for governmental provision.

But the battles over health care, education, and other goods under-way today express a very different view of public goods, one grounded not in economic terms of efficiency and production, but rather in moral and political concepts. In this framework, "public goods" are those essential to enabling human success and well-being. Let's call this the *democratic conception* of public goods. It is a democratic conception in the substantive and aspirational sense of "democracy": these are goods that we owe to one another in a shared democratic society. In turn, this suggests that ensuring equal access to these goods is a matter of public concern and public obligation.

Viewed this way, public goods encompass much more than conventional utilities and infrastructure (such as roads, bridges, and electricity). The category also includes a wider array of "social infrastructure"—those essentials that allow for one's full potential to be met, ranging from health care and housing to broadband Internet.

Such moral appeals to the importance of basic necessities and the need to provide them publicly and equally are familiar aspirations. But by themselves they have often been politically unpersuasive: skeptics frequently cast these demands as luxuries rather than necessities or argue that they would be too costly to provide publicly. And in an era marked by deep distrust in government, "self-correcting" free markets might seem more likely to provide such goods and services efficiently and competently.

But a democratic conception of public goods entails more than just the aspiration for equal access to basic necessities. It also includes a second, critical claim: that power in the modern economy is exercised through the control, administration, and provision of these very goods. Whether they are public agencies or private firms, providers of goods such as health care exercise control over those dependent on them. Historically this power has been used in ways that create and perpetuate racial and economic injustice. Public goods must be democratic, then, in a second sense: by ensuring the accountability and responsiveness of these providers and protecting beneficiaries of public goods from exploitation.

A democratic conception of public goods raises a related constitutive claim as well. The practical realities of who can access which goods, and on what terms, represent the codification and institutionalization of citizenship—or its denial. Access to these goods is one of the key ways our society defines the demos itself.

THE DEMOCRATIC CONCEPTION of public goods has historical roots. During the Gilded Age and the subsequent Progressive Era, the American economy was in the throes of a terrifying and painful transformation not unlike today. Industrialization generated tremendous new wealth and opportunities, but the upheaval also deepened poverty and inequality, creating crises of health, pollution, and dislocation. Many workers and communities suddenly found themselves struggling to survive and at the mercy of new forms of power, such as railroads or financiers, who dictated the fates of whole towns and sectors from afar.

As a result many Americans suddenly lacked reliable, safe, and affordable access to the basic necessities of life. The dairy industry, for example, was an area of concern for many Progressives. The logistics of delivering fresh milk to booming urban centers made access difficult, and the common business practice of adulterating milk with chalk and toxic chemical dyes (to improve its appearance) made it a mortal danger to many children.

Progressives looked to the idea of "public utilities" as a solution. Today we think of public utilities in narrow terms, such as electricity or telecom. But starting at the state and local level, reformers established utilities for everything from milk and ice to transportation and banking. In some cases, these charters converted the private provider into a state- or city-run entity, which is how modern municipal utilities started. But in others, policy reforms implemented something more tailored: varying degrees of state oversight and regulation to ensure that goods were provided fairly, safely, and cheaply. In the case of milk, for instance, Progressive Era reformers not only imposed safety standards, but also created urban distribution centers that subsidized the high cost of fresh milk.

The telecom industry was also radically reshaped during this period. As telephones became increasingly central to social and economic life, reformers engaged in a fierce political battle with private telecom monopolies over norms of nondiscrimination and equal access. By 1910 antidiscrimination rules—which required telecom companies to provide service to anyone who could afford it—were in place in nineteen states. As historian Bill Novak has argued, these Progressive Era clashes over industrial capitalism and regulation helped formulate much of our contemporary understanding and practice of democracy.

Progressive Era reformers outlined a conception of public goods that was democratic and distinctive in several key respects: it saw goods in moral terms, as necessities for human flourishing; it recognized that without public oversight, private actors could dominate certain sectors in ways that would subject communities to arbitrary pricing and barriers to access; and it employed often mundane regulatory tools at the local and national level to realize these aspirations.

Crucially, however, Progressives also framed the category of public goods, and the tools deployed to manage them, as necessarily fluid, evolving over time in response to changing technologies, social needs, and transformations in the marketplace. As Herbert Croly, Progressive founder of the *New Republic*, argued in 1909, "Conditions . . . vary radically in different industries; and the case of each industry should be considered in relation to its special conditions." And those conditions can change: a sector in which provision is at first cheap and equally accessible through private providers may become exploitative or monopolized, requiring greater governmental oversight—or vice versa: a good that is a luxury today may be a necessity tomorrow.

The recent battles over net neutrality and broadband access illuminate this latter point, as the lack of broadband Internet (once considered a luxury) plays an increasingly conspicuous role in isolating communities from commerce and economic opportunity. Moreover, as the Internet assumes the role of the modern-day public sphere, in which communication, protest, and debate take place, private control over the terms of access and the transmission of data between users creates the risk of unchecked, arbitrary power within our democracy.

This is precisely why so many modern-day advocates of racial and economic justice have sought to create public utility–style regulations that would bar Internet service providers (such as Verizon and Com-cast) from discriminating against some users, while also pushing for the creation of municipal broadband networks to connect underserved communities. The stakes here extend beyond cost to encompass fundamental freedoms. Without fair, cheap, safe, and universal access to certain goods—and without checks on private providers—individuals and communities can be excluded from the heart of social, economic, and political life. Public goods, in other words, are not so much about "free stuff" as they are about the "stuff that makes us free."

OF COURSE GOVERNMENT PROVISION of a public good can have negative results. Much of the public's distrust of regulation rests on the decades-long conservative critique of government as inefficient, overly costly, and likely to be corrupted by special interests. But the democratic view of public goods reminds us that private actors can be a source of exploitation and unaccountable power.

The water crisis in Flint, Michigan, offers a glaring example of this story. After years of budget crunches, the state government imposed emergency management on Flint, which in turn sought to cut costs by switching the city's primary water source to a private provider. But the failure to sufficiently treat the water resulted in skyrocketing levels of lead in the water, poisoning an entire community. Meanwhile the semi-privatizing of water in Flint has caused prices to spike, leading many residents to lose access altogether.

This story extends well beyond Flint: cash-strapped localities all over the country have moved to privatize their water utilities, raising similar concerns about safety, quality, pricing, and access. On average, water costs have skyrocketed by 40 percent over the last five years, a trend that could cause one-third of Americans to lose access to safe water by 2020.

The Flint crisis shows that what matters more than the identity of the goods provider—public or private—is the way in which the good is provided, and in particular, what its provision means for democratic values of access and accountability. In fact, the lived realities of public goods—how they are provided, who provides them, and to whom—represent some of the central ways in which we construct, perpetuate, and institutionalize economic and racial inequalities today.

Statements such as Mulvaney's are emblematic of a long-standing pattern of casting beneficiaries of certain public goods as "undeserving." In 1976 Ronald Reagan infamously popularized the pernicious stereotype of the "welfare queen," framing racial minorities as the fraudulent and indolent recipients of excessive government benefits at the expense of hard-working taxpayers. But attacks on the "undeserving" poor have a sadly bipartisan history. From paternalistic pre-industrial welfare systems to Clinton-era welfare reform, questioning whether certain populations "deserve" help has been a touchstone for liberal and conservative critiques of welfare.

This idea of deservingness has been institutionalized in the bureaucratic administration of public goods themselves. The New Deal, for example, deliberately excluded women and communities of color from many of its labor and safety-net protections. Today state governments can set requirements for receiving basic safety-net goods such as food stamps and welfare. As a result, many of these programs involve thousands of small barriers to entry that cumulatively restrict access to essential goods and services. The simple act of claiming an entitlement is often laden with punitive and pointless conditions, such as needlessly complex paperwork, strict reporting requirements, and demeaning interviews. Despite their nominally universal and enabling aspirations, these goods are instead administered to exclude and restrict.

At the local level, such exclusion is often achieved more literally by geographic restrictions. In the backlash against the civil rights movement, for example, wealthier and whiter communities routinely seceded from more diverse localities, forming their own municipal governments with separate systems for schools, parks, and other goods. The result has been de facto resegregation of access to high-quality public goods. These communities would rather withdraw from a large, public arena than make their goods and services available to all.

These exclusionary strategies are even more glaring when seen in the context of the many hidden forms of subsidization and support that wealthier communities receive. In the health care fight, for example, critics of expanded Medicaid or Medicare gloss over the degree to which most employer-backed plans are themselves subsidized by taxpayers.

Housing offers another example. The waiting list for the Housing Choice Voucher program (commonly known as Section 8, which offer subsidies for poor families to pay rent) is so long that some cities have simply stopped accepting new applicants. We could fully fund these vouchers for an estimated $25 billion annually. In comparison, we already subsidize housing for homeowners (mostly wealthier and whiter families) to the tune of $171 billion per year through the home mortgage interest deduction and other tax benefits.

Suzanne Mettler calls this the "submerged state," the embedding of governmental benefits in often-hidden provisions of the tax code. While such subsidies may be economically efficient in some respects, the result undermines support for public provision. After all, many beneficiaries of public support (such as those with home mortgage deductions) do not think of themselves as beneficiaries, thus allowing them to falsely valorize the free market and denigrate others as "undeserving" recipients of welfare.

This illusion of free-market efficiency and personal choice results in a predictable public goods death spiral. After initial pressures to cut taxes, local and state governments have been starved of revenue, which leads to declining budgets. This creates a justification for cutting services and outsourcing them to private contractors. Increasingly, these goods and services are also financialized—transferred to private equity investors who operate the services for profit, such as water in Flint or the private equity takeover of New York's ambulance services. But as private actors take on more and more power to exploit and extract, the same emaciation of governmental institutions, capacities, and personnel makes it ever less likely that these providers can be overseen effectively—or that goods can be made public again in the future.

Many of these exclusionary techniques are mutually reinforcing. The imposition of austerity budgets makes it easier to justify greater barriers to access. Racializing and villainizing the recipients of benefits makes it easier to cut budgets. Hiding the ways in which wealthier communities also receive public support further reduces potential support for universal and equitable access. These mechanisms comprise a sadly routine and durable playbook for constructing economic and racial exclusion.

SO FAR, this is a grim story. But we do in fact have the resources and tools to provide these public goods on universally accessible and democratic terms. To the extent that public goods are not provided universally, it is emphatically not because of a lack of resources or institutional capacity; it is rather because of a deliberate effort to hoard resources and access for some, exclude others, and shift responsibilities from public to private actors as a way of entrenching these distributions.

If exclusion is constructed in the administration and provision of public goods (by both public and private actors), the struggle for justice, economic freedom, and inclusion can therefore achieve much by focusing on bureaucracy.

Consider the case of housing. By some estimates, nearly 40 million households around the country are "rent-burdened," spending over 30 percent of their income on housing. Though clearly a public good in the democratic sense described earlier, housing is not recognized as an affirmative constitutional right. Yet if we were to expand regulatory and administrative oversight of the housing sector, we could come quite close to approximating housing as a public good.

In rapidly gentrifying cities, for example, a number of important proposals are currently on the table. Reformers in New York have proposed greater regulation of the rental market, requiring a licensing system for landlords or "certificates of no-harassment" that prove landlords have not forced out current tenants before they are permitted to sell their properties. Instead of huge tax breaks to developers to encourage construction, Section 8 vouchers and other rent subsidies could also be radically expanded, and localities could provide seed land and funding for public projects. Bureaucratic enforcement of eviction could be dramatically reduced and made more tenant-friendly. Cities in the Bay Area are even considering bringing back rent control and rent stabilization.

Taken together, these provisions would effectively make housing a utility. It would still be private and would still generate return for landlords, but these returns would be modest. Furthermore, the capacity of landlords to exploit or harass tenants would be curtailed. Most importantly, housing would be more affordable and accessible as a result.

Similar strategies could also help restore the "publicness" of recently privatized goods, such as water in Michigan. For example, the Michigan

Human Right to Water Act, a legislative package introduced in 2015, contains provisions that would restrict prices, establish affirmative obligations for safety, impose regulatory restrictions on shutoffs, and mandate greater oversight by state agencies, including the creation of a water ombudsman. And despite the attacks on the safety net in national politics, local governments such as New York have successfully pioneered the creation of a new public good in the form of universal pre-K, an idea that is proliferating rapidly.

This return of public goods depends crucially on the role of government, and, in particular, administrative agencies at the local and national levels. But it need not rest on a Panglossian view of what government can do. Progressive Era reformers may have had an overly optimistic view of government, operating as they did at the dawn of the modern administrative state. But even then, the successes of Progressive Era (and later New Deal) administration owed much not just to bureaucrats but to the social movements that helped to empower and create it—and ultimately to keep it honest.

Today's task of achieving a democratic conception of public goods requires a similar effort. The FCC would not have established net neutrality, for example, without the tremendous mobilization and organizing by groups such as Color of Change and Fight for the Future. Nor would the Flint water crisis have reached national prominence without the work of activists on the ground.

It should be no surprise that efforts to reform public goods—from the water rights bill in Michigan to restoring investment in local parks, schools, and jobs programs—increasingly include measures to ensure the representation and accountability of both the government and private actors. The distribution of public goods, after all, has become another way in which we police democracy's borders, and the public at large has a real stake in these debates.

The brazenness of modern conservatism raises (and clarifies) the stakes. Thanks to conservative control of dozens of state legislatures, public functions are being privatized at an accelerated pace. At the federal level, the Trump administration wants to dismantle net neutrality as well as slash funding for Medicaid and housing. What is at stake is not only what we owe to each other, but who we are. By fighting to make the provision of these vital goods public and universal, we assert our commitment to a broadly inclusive "we." We help institutionalize and instantiate that imaginary community, making it real, tangible, meaningful, and—hopefully—durable.

The Third Rail

Elaine Kamarck

I AM CERTAINLY SYMPATHETIC to Sabeel Rahman's critique that there is "a long-standing pattern of casting beneficiaries of certain public goods as 'undeserving.'" Starting with Ronald Reagan's welfare queens, the recipients of public goods have often been demonized as unworthy in one way or another. This is especially upsetting given the plethora of government benefits—from mortgage deductibility to retirement savings accounts to college savings accounts—that accrue to the advantage of the upper middle class. It can be argued that the truly undeserving are the well-off Americans whose government largesse comes in the form of tax expenditures, not welfare checks.

Nonetheless, to ignore or dismiss the "underserving" argument is to miss an important ingredient of successful American public policy. Americans have always been strong individualists. This ethos goes back to the pioneer experience of settling a continent in an era when people had to rely on themselves and their immediate neighbors and when government was, for all practical purposes, nonexistent.

Although we are a long way from the pioneer era, a nation's DNA dies hard. A substantial number of Americans still glorify the individual and believe that it is everyone's responsibility to work hard and take care of their own. It's why, for instance, America has never had a successful socialist party while Europe has.

Progressive or liberal policy that ignores this strain in the public consciousness will always be vulnerable to the argument that government that takes from those who work and gives to those who do not is illegitimate. Fortunately policy that is constructed with an understanding of this tension can stand the test of time.

The best example is President Franklin D. Roosevelt's creation of Social Security. The Great Depression highlighted the need for a significantly more robust social safety net than America had ever had before. But in 1933, two years before Roosevelt and his secretary of labor, Frances Perkins, set to work designing a social safety net, Roosevelt created the Civilian Conservation Corps—a massive program that put people to work. It was a politically shrewd move, and one that was completely consistent with the value Americans place on work over "a handout."

Then, when Frances Perkins began to look for models for the safety net, she looked to prominent academics, including Russian immigrants such as Abraham Epstein and Isaac M. Rubinow. These two men dominated thinking in the policy community at the time. Epstein was the author of *Facing Old Age* (1922), which shaped thinking in the 1920s. Rubinow, an avowed socialist, founded the American Association for Old Age Security in 1927 and promoted the ideas of national health insurance and income maintenance for workers.

And yet, when it came time for Perkins to put together a team to enact social welfare legislation, neither Epstein nor Rubinow was called into the White House to participate (much to their dismay).

As the process unfolded, Roosevelt dumped many of the ideas that had been near to the hearts of these reformers—including national health insurance.

Roosevelt understood that he needed to create a uniquely *American* social safety net—one that tapped into the deep reservoir of individualism that lay underneath the American psyche and one that avoided, at all costs, the appearance of a "dole." As a result, the architecture of the two social safety net programs that survived, unemployment insurance and old-age insurance, evolved in a substantially different direction than similar programs in Europe.

The unemployment compensation program was given to the states to run, reflecting the prevailing (and current) belief in localism that is so much a part of U.S. political culture. And both programs, unemployment insurance and the old-age pension (what we now know as Social Security), were structured as insurance programs. In both instances, taxes were deducted from the payroll and, unlike in Europe, only citizens who had contributed to the system could get benefits.

The result was most definitely not to the liking of the reformers who had come from or who looked to Europe for their inspiration. But Roosevelt knew what he was doing. Because the structure was uniquely American in its values, it was able to survive. As he explained:

> These taxes were never a problem of economics. They were politics all the way through. We put these payroll contributions there so as to give the contributors a legal, moral and political right to collect their unemployment benefits. With these taxes in place no damn politician can ever scrap my social security program.

The genius of Roosevelt was to create a social safety net that was based on a familiar model—the insurance model—and that tapped into the

American values of individualism and hard work. Social welfare benefits were to be "earned," not simply given out by the government. This clever distinction meant that the changes survived even as Republicans attempted to undo the New Deal. By 1952 a popular Republican president, Dwight D. Eisenhower, made it clear that his party would no longer try to unravel the signature safety net program of the New Deal.

In subsequent years the program was expanded to include dependents, survivors, and even the disabled, and it has been responsible for a dramatic drop in poverty among the elderly. No wonder it remains unparalleled in its popularity and has been called "the third rail of American politics" because of the potential damage to any politician who dares oppose it.

American social reformers working in other countries, especially developing countries, make a great (albeit not always successful) effort to be culturally sensitive in their work. But reformers working on American social programs do not often internalize the same lesson. While Rahman is correct to point out that the bureaucratic administration of the welfare state often consists of too many barriers to entry, it is critical to understand that many of these barriers are rooted in America's culture and morality. If we are more culturally sensitive in the American context, then we can build, as Roosevelt did, sustainable public goods.

Saving the Commons from the Public

Michael Hardt

SABEEL RAHMAN'S ARGUMENT against the privatization of public goods and services contributes to a rich stream of contemporary critiques of neoliberalism that rightly focuses on how privatization creates and maintains forms of exclusion and hierarchy. In response to privatization, Rahman calls to make public goods public again—that is, to design and bolster government programs that foster social inclusion and equality, broadening both our conception of public goods and the populations whose membership grants them access to those goods.

Rahman's argument, however, rests on a notion of the opposition between public and private that obscures the full range of political possibilities. Indeed, many critiques of neoliberalism assume that the only solution is a return to economic projects of Keynesian state control, usually combined with political discourses of classical liberalism (Rahman's primary touchstone is the Progressive Era). Older notions of state provision and regulation may well be preferable to the neoliberal rule of private property, but they carry their own forms of exclusion and injustice. Rahman himself recognizes the history of racial and gender hierarchies embedded in state structures of public goods. One might add the exclusion of migrants and indigenous populations, among others, from membership in the political community.

Fortunately the private and the public are not our only options. The common—defined by open access to, and shared democratic management of, social wealth—provides an alternative. In fact, Rahman's argument points at times, ambiguously, in the direction of the common.

I will offer some examples of how social wealth can be shared as common, but before I do that, I want to address some basic conceptual distinctions, the first of which regards the nature of property. For the purposes of this discussion, I adopt the commonsense understanding of private property as defined by the right to exclude others and exert a monopoly over decision-making. It is true that modern private property, as every first-year law student will tell you, is characterized not by an absolute right of ownership, but by a bundle of rights such that ownership is conditioned by others affected by property. Such plurality, however, is always restricted and does not alter the ultimate authority and power of exclusion afforded by ownership.

Furthermore, public ownership, by which I understand state regulation and control, does not fundamentally alter the basic exclusions of property. More people may have access to public property than private property, but the state retains the right to decision-making and restricts access to those who "belong." Rahman calls this power the codification and institutionalization of membership—or its denial. The public, in other words, maintains its own forms of monopoly over access and decision-making. Indeed private and public frequently function together to maintain exclusions and hierarchies. For example, many authors have detailed how public housing projects in the United States have not lessened the racial segregations created by private property but instead reinforced them.

The common, in contrast to both the private and the public, is defined by open access and democratic decision-making. It thus designates not a third kind of property, but a non-property structure for sharing social wealth.

Second, by invoking the common I do not intend to harken back to precapitalist social arrangements that were destroyed by the enclosures, but to indicate new means for sharing social wealth today. I also reject tragedy-of-the-commons style objections, which claim that unmanaged social wealth, such as a field for grazing, will inevitably come to ruin and that the only effective means of management are private ownership or state control. Such preemptive objections serve as a red herring that closes down debate. The common of course must be managed, but a politics of the common rests on the wager that shared social wealth can be managed democratically, outside of either private or public control.

Third, distinguishing the public from the common is critical, since in English (and many other languages) the term "public" is ambivalent, referring in some usages to state control and in others to the common. When one refers to a reading *public*, for instance, or to making one's ideas *public*, the "public" in question refers primarily to the common. This ambivalence of standard usage conceals an important divide between circumstances under which state decision-making and the state's powers of exclusion are central versus those under which decision-making is democratic and access open and equal. In discussions of public property and public goods, I thus use the term "public" only in reference to the state, so that the common can come into view.

Rahman's discussions of the public are ambivalent in the way I have just outlined. Whereas in the major portion of the essay he addresses state provision and regulation of public goods, a minor line of argumentation gestures toward the common. For example, lamenting the unequal distribution in the United States of access to safe water, health care, and housing, he calls for a more broadly inclusive "we." Presumably, access would then be open equally to all, including migrants and all previously excluded populations.

Rahman's call for a newly democratic conception of public goods could also point toward the common, assuming this would oppose any monopoly of decision-making, private or public. That assumption suggests a final conceptual point: differentiating the common from the public requires a distinct understanding of democracy. Rahman seems to conceive of democracy in terms of just and responsible structures of representation, highlighting the accountability and responsiveness of public officials. The common, in contrast, requires a fuller notion of democracy in which all participate in making decisions about access to and management of social wealth. It is beyond the scope of this short piece to debate the feasibility of such a participatory notion of democracy; my point is that how we define democracy is central to questions of public goods and the common.

All these conceptual distinctions are salient in contemporary social movements that demand a right to the common. Just as Rahman claims housing is a right, so too does the Spanish *Plataforma de Afectados por la Hipoteca* (Platform of Those Affected by Mortgages), known as the PAH. Whereas Rahman proposes public means, such as rent control and rent subsidies, to create greater access and counter the neoliberal powers of finance and gentrification, the PAH defends the right to housing through various forms of social action and civil disobedience: the group not only protects those threatened with eviction or utility shut-offs, but also occupies empty apartments owned by banks to provide housing to the homeless. The PAH does engage the state—for instance, to demand reforms of housing laws and the enlargement of laws that defend renters' and debtors' rights—but its center of gravity resides in the common, not in the public. It seeks to make housing available to all through democratic decision-making structures.

The Dakota Access Pipeline protests at Standing Rock illuminate another face of the common. Led by an extraordinary gathering of North American tribes, the movement did not contest the pipeline route based on property rights. Nor did it appeal for greater state regulation or control. It posed a much more fundamental challenge, the implications of which extend well beyond the issue of pipelines: a new relation to the earth—to view the earth as common and to develop practices of care and participation on that basis. To share the earth in this way would require a radical transformation of the current social order.

Social movements such as the PAH and the pipeline protests render visible the common, which is so often obscured in discussions of public goods. They demonstrate that the public is not the only means of combatting neoliberal privatization and open up a wider range of social and political alternatives.

Rahman astutely notes that what is at stake in the debate is not only the distribution of social wealth but also the production of subjectivity: *who* we are. Neither the private nor the public, however, will ever produce the "broadly inclusive 'we'" he aims for. Genuine inclusion and social equality can only be constructed through the open access and democratic participation that characterize the common.

All Good Things
Jacob T. Levy

IN ORDER TO RESPOND to Sabeel Rahman's essay, I begin with some distinctions in terminology, the significance of which I will make clear later. The following labels are not meant to do any argumentative work by themselves; the important thing is the distinctions they make.

Public goods: While Rahman uses it more broadly, let's reserve this for the traditional economics definition, goods that are nonexcludable and nonrivalrous. These are "consumed" individually: I like clean air, and so do you, and so does that person, but we each breathe it separately. The justification behind coercive provision is the aggregate benefit to all of the consumers: if the good could be normally bought and sold, its price as determined by market forces would be higher than the cost of providing it via public action.

Social goods: These are goods with significant returns to scale, sometimes because of straightforward network effects (a telephone increases in value when more people have telephones) and sometimes for more complicated reasons. A bus system is not *simply* a network good; at a given level of bus service, having more passengers makes riding less attractive, not more. But if having more passengers makes it more cost-effective to increase service, which increases the frequency that buses can run, which makes buses a more attractive transportation option, which attracts more passengers, then the whole virtuous cycle is something like a network effect. Here, enjoyment is not only aggregative: it is not that I like riding the bus or using a telephone, and so do you, and so does that person. When we all do so, we get more out of it. We are still individual consumers, but we benefit from each other's consumption.

Communal goods: While social goods can often shape a whole community, as both communications technology and transportation do, that is not their core purpose. By contrast, within any association, society, or organized group—voluntary or ascriptive, public or private—there are buildings, spaces, celebrations, events, artwork, or rituals that have as a primary purpose the affirmation of the community as a community, signaling continuity with the past, shared membership, something about the community's meaning or identity, and so on. Civic architecture and monuments may be like this, but so are a congregation's church or temple and a university's expensive graduation ceremony. We think of these the wrong way if we imagine conducting a poll of the members and asking, "What would you have been willing to pay for an admissions ticket? Are you getting your money's worth?" The association or community aims to provide these in a way that *shapes* their members' preferences and values, rather than only *responding* to them: a monument that generates patriotism, a synagogue that inspires devotion, a graduation that cements loyalty to the alma mater.

Necessities and dignity goods: These are ordinary goods whose production and sale are uncomplicated, and that are consumed or enjoyed by individuals who may either depend on the goods for survival or because, in Adam Smith's words, "the custom of the country renders it indecent for creditable people, even of the lowest order, to be without" them. Smith used the example of linen shirts and leather shoes, which in his time, though not a matter of life or death, were necessary to go out in public without shame. Smith considered all such good to be necessities, "not only those things which nature, but those things which the established rules of decency have rendered necessary to the lowest rank of people."

It seems to me that Rahman's essay deliberately effaces these distinctions, drawing very different kinds of goods under a unified label, with the effect of letting each of the reasons that exist for communal or public provision reinforce each other and seem to apply to all the relevant cases. Necessities become communal goods, not only because access to them shores up dignity or prevents starvation, but because they ensure equality among citizens, defining "the demos itself." But a person's reasons for wanting to be decently fed, clothed, and housed are reasons they have *as a person*. And in a basically functional market economy in which he or she has sufficient income, the person *will* be decently fed, clothed, and housed. If the person does not have sufficient income, he or she will suffer both deprivation and shame, but those are no more losses qua citizen than they are qua family member, congregant, neighbor, or any other social role or position. Each of an individual's communities has some reason to help him or her reach a basic threshold, but the polity no more than any other. And as acutely as one feels hunger or the shame of being badly clothed, the absence of food or clothing is symptomatic of the lack of money. If everyone has enough income, then food, housing, and clothing can be ordinary consumer goods—*and nothing is gained by treating them otherwise*. Mixing up the human need not to starve with the needs of democratic citizenship gives the deprivation both too little human value *and* too much symbolic weight.

What do we want in the provision of a good? Is it sufficiency, equality, progress, or simply *more*? Different answers to these questions call for genuinely different kinds of responses. If we want sufficiency, as we do with dignity goods and necessities, very often we should not pay much attention to the provision of the goods themselves; we should pay attention to the problem of poverty, and worry about economic growth, barriers to entering the labor market, redistribution and poverty relief, or some combination of these. (Direct public provision of food, or indirect provision through food stamps, is certainly not better for recipients' dignified membership in the community than their having enough money to be able to simply afford food.)

If we want progress over time, it will often be necessary to allow inequality at each point in time, as technological or organizational innovations are experimented with at the more expensive end of a market, some of them diffusing out. This is true even of public goods, which are defined as a kind of technical organizational problem. Sometimes such problems can be solved, as new techniques become available; electronic toll collection (E-ZPass and similar systems) makes it much easier and less disruptive to introduce excludability and pricing to roads, for example. If you imagine a particular necessity or access to a social good becomes so inexpensive relative to incomes that it can be had very easily, there is no problem left. The same is true if the organizational difficulties that define public goods happen to be solvable in some case. If these problems disappear and the goods become ordinary consumer goods thanks to innovation, so much the better.

None of this is true for communal goods. (If you prefer, when thinking of the specifically political subset of these, think of them as *civic* goods.) They are not technical problems to solve, or individual needs to be met. Their aim is to affirm shared membership and meaning. But in seeing them plainly that way, we can understand that they are also open to entirely legitimate challenge and contestation. Public monuments, memorials, celebrations, and spaces make claims about particular meanings, and they are often meanings that we should be arguing about: Columbus Day, or statues commemorating the Confederacy, to take familiar examples. Communal goods like this are not individually consumed, and should not benefit from the halo effect of the provision of, for example, necessities. In demanding that such a statue be taken down I am not proposing to take food out of a neighbor's mouth. Making the provision of ordinary goods *civic* and tying it closely to the demos thus tends to make contestation over the genuinely communal or civic sphere more difficult. It attaches a symbolic character to the democratic state as the source of all good and necessary things that it should not carry.

State actors are generally all too happy to have the people they rule believe that kind of thing. In an era of populist nationalism and incipient authoritarianism, I think we need to be concerned about how to keep people's attention on the *plurality* of memberships that they have, the plurality of productive systems from which they benefit, the plurality of provisions they receive. Those who come to believe that all good things come from their membership in the demos believe something nationalistic and false, for example, about their country's relationship to international and global trade. Those who believe their membership in the demos is constitutive of their social dignity believe something nationalistic and false about direct horizontal connection in civil society. We can take seriously the communal goods of democratic government without seeking to symbolically collapse our subnational and transnational connections and interdependences—through the market as well as through civil society—into a hypertrophied sense of the importance of political membership and provision.

Naming the Villain

Lauren Jacobs

SABEEL RAHMAN'S ESSAY is a call to action. Progressives should take seriously the coming political struggle over public goods generally and infrastructure specifically. They should also be better skilled in the administration of government and learn how to use the tools available to incrementally transform the material conditions of our current system. But as a lifelong organizer, dedicated to the dignity and economic security of all workers, I know that this is not enough. It is also critical that we see the big picture: the corporate power and its accompanying dogma of the supremacy of profit that brought us to this brink. They are the enemies we face. And they must be named. From fairy tales such as Rumpelstiltskin, to J. K. Rowling's Harry Potter series, many of the stories of our childhood teach us the same lesson: we must name the villain before we stand any chance of defeating it.

Any discussion of public goods is ultimately a discussion of values. How we define who is included in the notion of a "public"—and what we think is in the best interest of that public—are inherently political and therefore always contested. Those definitions live at the intersection of race, wealth, gender, and work.

Infrastructure is simply the structures on which a society depends to function. Yet the word frequently calls to mind a narrow set of images, roads, bridges, and white male construction workers chief among them. The many women and people of color who work in health care, education, and transit are not the workers we associate with infrastructure. And yet, society needs schools, hospitals, parks, public transit, and clean affordable water just as much as it needs well-tended roads. This misconception of what infrastructure means makes the work of certain people invisible, in much the way we have long made invisible their private work, from the domestic to childcare.

There is only a fraction of society with minimal reliance on these public services. The wealthy often send their children to private schools, seldom take public transportation, have access to private hospitals and health institutions, and even live in communities that purchase commercially processed water. However, these elites do still rely on roads and bridges for logistics and the transportation of commerce. It is little surprise then that the outsized power this class exerts over our government means that *these* public goods are maintained even in thin times.

One of the greatest threats that faces our public goods is privatization. Although Rahman comments on the points of tension surrounding private finance, privatization, and austerity, he does not fully outline the playbook that private finance uses to convince governments and people to surrender the disbursement of public goods to the for-profit sector. The process almost always looks something like this: 1) taxes are cut to allegedly spur job growth; 2) as a result, government budgets are smaller; 3) needing to reduce spending, jobs and services are cut; 4) in addition, certain racial groups are blamed for using more than their fair share of public services; 5) because of the cuts lower quality service is provided; and 6) because of this failure to deliver acceptable outcomes, government is said to need more efficient management, such as that found in the private sector.

What do we know about the corporate elites and wealthy who create and benefit from this cycle of manufactured scarcity? Their business practices—and the government policies that buttress these, which they purchase through lobbying—benefit only a tiny sliver of the population and have wreaked financial devastation on the majority. They know that these business practices and policy ideas are not supported by a majority of the electorate and have therefore resolved to support administrative disenfranchisement tools (felon disenfranchisement, voter ID laws, the reduction of early voting, opposition to same-day registration, and gerrymandering) to make sure that legislative- and executive-branch power is maintained by politicians and political blocs that are friendly to these practices. What's more, their spokespeople regularly use racist, misogynist, and homophobic tropes, both subtle and blatant, to justify the continuation of this agenda.

In short, we must abandon the false belief that where and how to invest in the public good is a civic *or* civil debate. We do not share goals with our opponents; they do not want a more just distribution of income, an expanded electorate, or to increase the power that ordinary citizens have to influence government. We are confronting economic interests that ruthlessly seek new sources of revenue and income and will happily do so at the cost of our democracy. This is ultimately a struggle for freedom and the people's pursuit of happiness.

Some blame the Republican Party for this state of affairs. This is incorrect, not only because there exists a robust roster of Democratic politicians who are equally culpable, but also because it is a form of misdirection: it fails to recognize those who receive financial benefit from the arrangement. Corporations in every state have colluded—via think tanks, direct political influence, and even the economic blackmail of threatening to move their headquarters—to produce the governments they wish for and that the rest of us must live with.

Conversations are often torturously twisted just to avoid mentioning the names of these anonymous influencers. Consider how often you heard the name Nestlé in conversations about the Flint water crisis—yet while Flint residents still wait for clean water, Nestlé continues to extract 150–200 gallons a minute of groundwater from Michigan. For this multibillion-dollar extraction, Nestlé pays the state just $200 a year. How often are the names of the large health insurance corporations, such as Aetna, Humana, or Cigna —those that extract billions of dollars in profit every year from keeping the system broken—brought up in the discussion of our health care crisis?

How do we start? When the next unfit charter school is uncovered, let us flood the offices of not only the Department of Education, but also those of the hedge fund companies, such as Greenlight Capital, that have funded the school privatization movement. We can expose the heartlessness of those who want to use our children for their free-market experiments. When the next city is poisoned by lead in the water, let us visit the shareholders of the private management companies that peddle poisoned water, as well as the offices of local government. We can expose how the bottom line often takes precedence over the health of our families. By directly confronting those who have placed their wealth above our health, we will shape "we, the people" as a broader, more diverse, and inclusive coalition. This new "we" can hold all of us who believe that the preciousness of life and freedom should never be trumped by profit.

There are four strategies we can deploy to seize the challenge of this moment:

1) *Name and fight the profiteers:* Several large-scale investors, such as the Blackstone Group, are poised to invest heavily in—and therefore potentially privatize—the nation's bridges, roads, transit systems, and other critical

infrastructure. Our campaigns need to name these entities and look for weak points where we can challenge their power.

2) *Fight for and win the infrastructure that society needs:* We need to center the voices of our diverse citizenry to decide the structures that are needed in our communities. We should embrace the aspirational and be undaunted by being labeled unrealistic. A compelling vision of what could and should be will inspire.

3) *Build power:* Beyond merely mobilizing residents for hearings, we need to consider how our work builds long-term power for our movement. Are there more people involved than when we began? Are those people better able to engage others and bring them into this work? Organizing on a massive scale is critical. Activism around infrastructure provides a great opportunity to do this: everyone cares about water, hospitals, and schools.

4) *Use all of our available tools* to expand the definition of what is considered a public good.

And as Rahman suggests, where we govern, we need to govern well and strategically.

This political moment calls on us to reach and strive for the most just and equitable society we can imagine. To do this means confronting the true obstacles we face. It is perhaps best said by Rowling's character of Albus Dumbledore, the headmaster of Hogwarts: "Always use the proper name for things. Fear of a name increases fear of the thing itself."

A Beautiful Public Good

Joshua Cohen

SABEEL RAHMAN'S DEMOCRATIC CONCEPTION of public goods is founded on the idea of a public responsibility for ensuring the essentials of
a democratic society. Public goods are among those essentials. They
answer to the basic needs of persons, conceived of as free and equal
members of a democratic society. What those public goods are and the
best methods for providing them vary across time and circumstance.
In our time and circumstance, public goods should include clean water
and air, good schools, broadband Internet access, and quality health
care. Discharging the responsibility to provide those goods is not only
a core public responsibility, Rahman says. It will also help to foster a
sense of commonality—of a *we* with a common fate. Rahman calls this
dimension of public provision the "constitutive" aspect of public goods.

I agree with much of Rahman's view, but found his account of this
constitutive aspect surprisingly thin. In a collaborative spirit, I propose to
thicken this aspect of the democratic conception with a story about how the
ambition to foster democracy and democratic sensibilities helped to shape
the design of Central Park, one of the country's truly great public goods.

IN A 1924 BIOGRAPHY of Frederick Law Olmsted, Broadus Mitchell says that Olmsted was "first, and last, a democrat." A commitment to democracy links Olmsted's remarkable artistry in designing New York's Central Park with his early work as a journalist.

Olmsted spent much of 1853–54 working in the South. Then in his early thirties, Olmsted was writing for the *New York Daily Times* (eventually renamed the *New York Times*). Olmsted's journalism grew from arguments about slavery with his abolitionist friend Charles Loring Brace: "I am not a red-hot abolitionist like Charley, but am a moderate free soiler . . . would take in a fugitive slave and shoot a man that was likely to get him." Unconvinced by Brace's "red-hot" abolitionism, Olmsted decided to study southern agriculture, slavery, and white planter aristocracy close-up.

Olmsted's journalism eventually resulted in three books, synthesized in *The Cotton Kingdom* (1861). In the first, Olmsted writes: "Thus slavery, or aristocracy, a ruling or a subject class in a community, is in itself a very great hindrance to its industrial progress; that is, to its acquisition of wealth—*moral, aesthetic, and mental, as well as material wealth* [emphasis added]. This is the way Democrats reason."

Reasoning with the democrats, Olmsted rejected slavery and aristocracy. But he was an anxious democrat, worried about a powerful set of intellectual and practical challenges to democracy. Meeting those challenges would demand the full devotion of its adherents.

Olmsted expresses his anxieties in a letter to Brace in December 1853. Traveling with his older brother, John, he visited Samuel Perkins Allison, a Yale classmate of John's, large Tennessee planter, and "a thorough Aristocrat." Allison challenged the Olmsteds' democratic convictions: "he silenced us." Olmsted did not admire aristocrats, who cleaved to a conventional code of honor and lacked a genuine moral sense. But observing the shortcomings of aristocrats did not silence concerns about northern democracy, which was marked by poverty, toil, urban squalor, and a crude commercialism and materialism.

Shaken by Allison's challenge, Olmsted resolved: "I must either be an Aristocrat or more of a Democrat than I have been—a Socialist Democrat." As the phrase "socialist democrat" suggests, Olmsted was concerned with "a democratic condition of society," not only with a democratic form of government. Being more of a democrat, then, meant devoting himself to creating great public goods, including parks and other public spaces, that would produce a "general elevation of all classes."

A few years later, in September 1857, Olmsted became superintendent of Central Park. Soon thereafter, he and Calvert Vaux won the contest to design the park. For Olmsted, designing Central Park was an opportunity to pursue the socialist-democratic ambition crystallized by his experience in the South. That ambition imposed three demands—all powerfully illustrated by Central Park and instructive about the democratic importance of public goods.

First, building Central Park meant expanding an opportunity to all that was then available only to the few. Olmsted once described the purpose of Central Park as "supply[ing] to the hundreds of thousands of tired workers, who have no opportunity to spend their summers in the country, a specimen of God's handiwork that shall be to them, inexpensively, what a month or two in the White Mountains or the Adirondacks is, at great cost, to those in easier circumstances." Ensuring great *public* spaces—making them available to all—served the value of *fairness*, and was thus a "political duty of grave importance."

But not just that. Central Park needed to be great, not simply open and available to all. It needed, in particular, to be *beautiful*.

Olmsted discerned a shared human interest in the experience of natural beauty. In his 1865 report on "Yosemite and the Mariposa Grove," he says:

> It has always been the conviction of the governing classes of the old world that it is necessary that the large mass of all human communities should spend their lives in almost constant labor and that the power of enjoying beauty either of nature or of art in any high degree, requires a cultivation of certain faculties, which is impossible to these humble toilers. . . . It is the folly of laws which have permitted and favored the monopoly by privileged classes of many of the means supplied in nature for the gratification, exercise and education of the esthetic faculties that has caused the appearance of dullness and weakness and disease of these faculties in the mass of the subjects of kings. And it is against a limitation of the means of such education to the rich that the wise legislation of free governments must be directed.

Making a beautiful public space available to all would thus answer to and awaken a shared human interest, suppressed but not extinguished by the "governing classes." As the Central Park Commission affirmed in its 1863 report, "there is a universality in nature."

Moreover, Central Park was not only about fair access to a great good. It was fostering social integration by bringing people together for a *shared* experience of that great good. "Democratic Government," Olmsted said, has a duty to provide "places and times for reunions, which shall be so attractive that the rich and the poor, the cultivated and well-bred, and the sturdy and self-made people shall be attracted together and encouraged to assimilate." Central Park thus needed to be a place for the people, and not simply for persons, and thus help to shape a sense of a *we*.

Designed with this constitutive aspiration, Central Park aimed to bring people together on an equal footing for a shared experience of natural beauty. The main locus of that experience was the Avenue, the park's great, open, public promenade—the "central feature" of the design—leading from the southern end of the park to the Bethesda Terrace, with its Alhambra-inspired, encaustic tile ceiling, and the densely wooded Ramble: the intersection of democracy and beauty. "Of all its great achievements and features," Park Commissioner Gordon Davis wrote in 1981, "there is none more profound or dramatically moving than the social democracy of this public space. For years it has been and today continues to be socially and racially integrated, notwithstanding patterns of caste and class stratification and polarization throughout society as a whole."

Blending fair access, natural beauty, and sociality, this great public good would refute the aristocrats. Their conviction—from Plato to the "governing classes of the old world" to southern aristocrats such as Samuel Perkins Allison—was that democracies aspire to do things for everyone and deliver lowest-common-denominator junk. That is why the "conspirators" trusted in 1861, "as they have ever trusted, to the supposed superiority of a community of privileged classes over an actual democracy." A compelling refutation of this aristocratic conceit needed to be practical: build a beautiful public good, trust that people would come, and have confidence that when they did, they would develop a sense of being a *we*—the people to whom the democratic park belonged.

The Last Word

K. Sabeel Rahman

THROUGHOUT THIS FORUM, the idea of public goods has been linked to water, housing, parks, and more. Taken together, the thoughtful responses highlight two crucial questions about our understanding of public goods. First, what types of goods qualify as "public" in a democratic conception? Or, more precisely, what makes a good "public," as opposed to merely ordinary? And second, what kinds of policy tools—including but not limited to direct state provision—can we employ to ensure more equitable and inclusive access to these goods?

I share Michael Hardt's attraction to the idea of the commons as a way to understand the moral aspirations of democratic public goods—goods that are open access and democratically governed. "Publicness," then, helps label those goods which are so vital that they *ought* to be governed with a focus on precisely these values of openness, access, and democratic control.

It is this publicness that animates Joshua Cohen's moving discussion of Frederick Law Olmsted and Central Park. For contemporary social reformers, parks served a critical public and democratic function by not only being accessible to all (and thereby dislodging aristocratic monopolization of ecological beauty) but also by creating a shared democratic experience through which a common identity as members of the polity could be constructed. Both Hardt and Cohen highlight what I think of as the *positive* dimension of democratic public goods: public goods enable new forms of individual and collective experience. In short, they empower individuals and communities.

But there is also a negative dimension that helps inform our identification of which goods should be accorded this moral stature of "publicness." Public goods are also those for which an *absence* of democratic control to ensure access is likely to place individuals and communities under troubling conditions of subordination. This was one of the key arguments in the rise of public utility regulation in the late nineteenth and early twentieth centuries.

Paralleling the positive, constructive visions of municipal reformers such as Olmsted, many reformers were energized by a wariness toward private actors who could exercise unchecked control over increasingly vital services such as telecom or railroads. These private actors, reformers argued, were essentially semi-sovereign, dictating the prospects of so many towns, businesses, and individuals without the democratic checks and balances that we expect of state actors. As Lauren Jacobs rightly argues in her essay, this same concern is present today: hedge funds and corporate actors continue to limit access to public goods.

These two conditions—the positive capacities that public goods can unlock, and the negative threat of domination if goods are governed undemocratically—help us identify a set of goods that deserve a heightened degree of scrutiny and attention.

While this set of goods is necessarily fluid and contested—changing with social, economic, and technological conditions—it is not unbounded. Jacob T. Levy is correct to point out that a broad understanding of public goods risks blurring different types of goods (particularly network-effect goods such as telecom, inputs into communal identity such as monuments, and basic necessities such as housing or health care); it is very much the case that not all goods can or should be considered "public" in quite the same way.

The related concern that Levy raises is in part an understandable fear of collapsing the plurality of human life and memberships into some monolithic notion of "publicness." Yet I am more sanguine than Levy here, in part because I see this broad moral notion of "publicness" operating differently. Rather than inexorably collapsing social and economic life into some monolithic, statist control over the market, a commitment to democratic public goods, defined broadly along the positive and negative dimensions, instead *enables* a plurality of life choices and opportunities. Goods such as housing and water are "public" precisely because they free individuals and communities to pursue more diverse paths.

This empowering, enabling aspect of public goods represents its own distinctly American tradition. Elaine Kamarck rightly notes that social policies are more durable when they can connect with deep traditions and shared values. But I would disagree with Kamarck that the only value capable of sustaining collective commitment to public goods and services is the concept of earned benefits. Certainly this is one aspect of American individualism, but we make a mistake if we overplay distinctions of deservingness in shaping our access to these goods.

Social Security and Medicare, which Kamarck cites as examples of individualism channeled into support for social policy, only came to be seen as shared, universal commitments through a concerted battle. They came to be universal precisely because post–New Deal bureaucrats employed ideas of equality and shared citizenship as a way to guide their decisions when administering those programs—and in some cases, resisting efforts to reassert racial disparities in access to benefits. Programs such as welfare, in contrast, gradually became more exclusionary precisely because administrators instead saw their work through the lens of deservingness and exclusion.

There is a different but equally American tradition in which to root this democratic conception of public goods: the conviction that we each deserve the opportunity to choose our own path. Threats to that freedom of self-authorship, whether originating from an oppressive state or a dominating private power, are threats to the American promise of freedom. This is the anxiety and aspiration that motivated Progressive Era innovators of public utility regulation. Thinkers such as Louis Brandeis and John Dewey saw themselves as pursuing reforms that would restore Founding-era values of individualism, liberty, and democracy.

This conception of public goods also suggests the importance of public policy in constructing access. Hardt suggests that we need not default to a statist notion of top-down control. While I share that view to an extent, regulation is key to overcoming many of the current barriers and ensuring fair and equal access—even if we aspire to manage public goods as a commons, rather than top-down state provision.

It remains the case, as Jacobs's essay points out, that access to public goods is controlled by both governmental and private actors, and increasingly, private actors operate these goods with a profit motive. Guaranteeing equal access thus requires surfacing these realities of power and control, and devising rules to make certain that such control is not overly concentrated or exclusionary. As Jacobs notes, this means tackling the role of hedge funds in driving school privatization, or taking on the alliances between large corporations and governmental regulators that contributed to the disinvestment in clean water in Flint.

Raising incomes and reducing poverty, as Levy suggests, is not sufficient in this fight: without a closer look at exactly how public and private actors own, govern, and administer these services, we are likely to leave many constituencies excluded. Net neutrality is an instructive example here: maintaining equal access of content providers and users to the Internet requires nondiscrimination regulations to prevent providers from favoring some kinds of content or excluding some constituencies.

Like the Progressive Era reformers, we should be experimenting with a range of regulatory tools to ensure equal access. We might, for instance, require common carriage or nondiscrimination obligations, enforced by government oversight. Or we might require various modes of democratic accountability and participation in governance regimes. We might even create "public options," state-chartered provisions that exist alongside private versions of the same good (much like Olmsted's vision of Central Park and city property).

These solutions represent a more varied toolkit for securing common access to public goods, and they are the result of understanding public goods both as a moral obligation as well as an administrative challenge.

This brings us full circle, for it turns out that in order to achieve the high moral vision of inclusion we need to dig into the granular realities of private power and regulation. This is a challenge since it is hard to reveal the realities of hidden private control and even harder to mobilize reform around technical background rules. But historically this productive tension between high moral aspirations and granular administrative innovations has helped fuel many of the greatest achievements of American democracy, from municipal parks to Social Security. That is a powerful lesson—and inspiration—for our contemporary struggles.

The Role of the Negro in the Work of Art

Shane McCrae

America I shower in the bright-

est bathroom in the house but it's the bathroom

With the lowest water pressure   most of the time

Your mighty rivers dribble down my chest   and

Back   in "The Dry   Salvages" T. S. El-

iot describes   "the river with its car-

go of dead negroes,   cows and chicken coops"

Because the river is   like time Ameri-

ca a   "destroyer" and "preserver" and

Like time America it's swollen with what

You eat   most   of the time   I don't feel like

I'm getting clean   your rivers dribble in

Bright light   preserver and destroyer when

I am seen how   will I survive being seen

McCrae

A Make-Believe Nation

Craig Santos Perez

Honolulu, Hawaii

I drive through the industrial neighborhood:
ocean blue tarps and colorful tents cluster
like a coral reef amongst a shipwreck of
shopping carts and bikes. This encampment
is one of many across Hawaii, the state
with the highest homeless rate in the nation.
So many islanders barely surviving beyond
the frame of a tourist postcard. So many
families bankrupted by the high cost
of living in "paradise." I park in the nearby
lot of the Children's Discovery Center,
then unbuckle my daughter from her car seat.
After I pay the admission fees, she pulls me
by the hand to her favorite area: a make-believe
town with a post office, clinic, library, theater,
television studio, grocery store, and classroom.
As she plays, I make-believe a nation where all
of this is a pure public good, nonrivalrous
and nonexcludable. A nation where housing,

good government, and bread are no longer
privatized. A nation divested from the public
harms of border walls and military weapons.
When she tires, we return to our car. I drive,
more slowly, through the encampment. Soon,
without warning, real bulldozers, dump trucks,
cops, and state workers will enforce laws
that ban sitting and lying in public spaces.
They will sweep these makeshift homes
and vulnerable citizens off the sidewalk,
where a girl is now playing in an inflatable
plastic pool, surrounded by her parents.
She looks the same age as my daughter,
who has fallen asleep in her car seat
as I dream of a future commons.

Perez

Soon Scrap Heap

Sally Ball

Look at all that pollution over Tempe.
The sky and the freeway one color: cement,
like the fallen wheelbarrow
skidded up against the barrier
of the carpool lane
coated in its own adhesive chalk,
grey cough of commerce,
of "growth," the powder of delayed
but certain obsolescence crusts
its wooden handles, grooved and dry.
Like everything here, dry enough
(cracked, gaunt, reduced
to some dwindling pith—)
not being dust yet
amounts to citizenship,
still votes.

Oh! not everyone old
is dwindling pith! Here
we must depend
on *that*. Retirees,
the monsoons turned into haboobs,

right? You remember,
the creosote smell of the rain,
the glaze—

Can I make the joke about white chickens?

Shall we just keep staring into the rearview mirror,
the barrow upside down. . . oh look, the cops are stopping.

Ball

Are Bureaucracies a Public Good?

Bernardo Zacka

IT WAS MY SECOND WEEK volunteering at a publicly funded antipoverty agency, and the waiting room was in the only state I had ever witnessed it: crowded. People were here to apply for a range of public programs, including food stamps, fuel assistance, health services, and Head Start. Some had sunk into their chairs with a look of resignation. Others seemed more anxious, holding on nervously to folders or plastic bags filled to the brim with paperwork.

The heavy silence was ruptured by the voice of the receptionist, DeShawn, who alternated between addressing clients—"Please take a seat and fill out this form, someone will be with you shortly, ma'am"—and answering the phone, which never stopped ringing.

I was training to become a receptionist, and DeShawn was introducing me to the trade.

An elderly woman, visibly exasperated, walked up to the desk and told us that it was her third visit in as many days. She explained that she met with a case manager the day before and was instructed to come back with additional documents. Her eyes were tired and her voice plaintive.

DeShawn leaned forward at first, as if to create an intimate space in the midst of the crowded room, but then reclined away in his swivel chair—mindful, as he later told me, not to appear too approachable to others.

He took turns apologizing—"I am terribly sorry"—and reminding the client that there were rules to which he had to adhere—"I am not authorized to take your documents myself; you must schedule another appointment with the staff member you saw yesterday."

I witnessed a similar balancing act on my way to the water cooler, where I overheard a young mother inquire about the services that her disabled daughter might be entitled to. The caseworker nodded and risked a smile, encouraging the mother to open up and divulge more information, but then quickly bounced back to neutral efficiency mode as soon as the relevant facts had surfaced, perhaps thinking of those still stranded in the waiting room.

As the day went on, with clients succeeding one another and demands piling up, this balancing exercise continued too, becoming ever more intricate and artful. Between solicitude and professional distance, empathy and rule-following, attentiveness and speed, the line to walk as a frontline bureaucrat was rather thin.

AND YET FOR ALL THIS, it is not a compliment to be called a bureaucrat. The word evokes rigidity, insensitivity, coldness, lack of initiative, and, above all, rule-worship. These attributes are so ingrained in our collective imaginary that they have become definitional. According to the *New Oxford Dictionary of English,* a bureaucrat is not just "an official in a government department" but, more specifically, "one perceived as being concerned with procedural correctness at the expense of people's needs."

When I first took up the job, I thought I knew what I was getting myself into. I was conducting ethnographic research for what would become my book, *When the State Meets the Street: Public Service and Moral Agency* (2017), and I had chosen the agency because, as a nonprofit contracted by the state, it was emblematic of the new face of public service provision. In preparation I had read every novel on bureaucracy I could lay my hands on, from works by Franz Kafka to David Foster Wallace, and I had come mentally prepared for the soul-sucking tedium of standard operating procedures.

But fiction, so suggestive in describing bureaucracy from the outside, turned out to be a rather poor guide to bureaucracy from within. Instead of precise rules dictating my every move, I found myself having to contend with a range of demands that were both vague and competing, with little practical guidance on how to do so.

So what does good bureaucracy look like? If you think about any public good—infrastructure, defense, the environment, the market—chances are there lurks in the background a bureaucratic agency charged with drafting regulations, monitoring compliance, and enforcing penalties. Bureaucracy is often thought of as the instrument that we deploy in the service of the public good. But can we also speak of bureaucracy as a public good in its own right? What is its proper role in the everyday functioning of a democratic state, and how can we enable bureaucrats to live up to such a role?

These questions are especially relevant and primed for attention now, at a time when people have lost trust in their government and its policies. Ever since the election of Donald Trump to the presidency of the United States, bureaucracy has had a strange reversal of fortunes. It has gone from being a thorn in the side of democracy to being its saving grace. In the space of a few days following his inauguration, the media was awash with stories detailing how bureaucracy could stand up to government and serve as a bulwark against populism.

The very attributes of bureaucracy that had earned it condemnation from across the political spectrum—its alleged inertia and inefficiency, questionable claims to expertise, and lack of responsiveness to political control—had now become virtues. For some this was just a marriage of convenience: bureaucracy was as detestable as ever, but nevertheless preferable to the alternative now within sight. If poor implementation had wrecked good policies, it might now save us from bad ones.

But for others this shift entailed a newfound appreciation for bureaucracy: perhaps there was a sensible rationale behind red tape, technocracy, and an independent-minded administrative apparatus. A culture of bureaucratic autonomy, after all, is not something that can be activated at the press of a button. If we want bureaucracy to be committed to a mission independent of the ebbs and flows of politics, we must be ready to accept it even when the political pendulum swings our way. But how should we define such a mission? And how can we best see it achieved?

WE ARE OFTEN TEMPTED to think of bureaucracy as a tool that can be utilized by successive governments to achieve policy objectives. This vision presupposes a strict division of labor: elected representatives select policies, bureaucrats execute them. The former is a morally charged task, which involves weighing competing values and interests; the latter is a technical matter, which involves enacting directives faithfully and efficiently.

However attractive this picture of bureaucracy may seem, it is a wildly inaccurate account of how bureaucracies actually function. The text of the law is often ambiguous and riddled with conflicts. It lends itself to various interpretations, and can be "operationalized" in a variety of ways. Resolving such indeterminacies is not merely a technical challenge, but one that requires bureaucrats to prioritize certain values and interests over others. Moral and political decision-making continue well within bureaucratic agencies, as the meaning of the law is clarified and given practical countenance.

In addition to being indeterminate, it is important to recognize that policy statutes are also frequently incomplete. They generally specify *what* bureaucracies should do, without spelling out in great detail *how* they should do it. With respect to public policy, we must be concerned not just with what policies the state should pursue, but also with how the state ought to interact with those who are subject to its authority when enacting such policies. The first question is settled by and large in legislative chambers; the second is resolved in bureaucratic agencies.

Consider any policy selected through proper democratic procedures. Regardless of its content, its implementation will have to respond to a further set of normative demands. At the very minimum, we would want the policy to be enacted in a way that is efficient, fair, responsive to the needs of individual citizens, and respectful of them. How to interpret these various demands, how to apply them to specific cases, and how to resolve conflicts that arise between them are normative challenges that are intrinsic to the implementation process.

At the antipoverty agency, for example, my colleagues and I were constantly reminded by our direct supervisor that we catered to vulnerable clients who spent their days being kicked around from one administrative office to another. It was incumbent upon us, by contrast, to create a warm and welcoming environment, in which they were treated courteously and felt respected as individuals. The directives we received from the agency's headquarters, however, said nothing about warmth or dignity. They emphasized the importance of retaining professional distance and serving clients on the basis of clear rules and standards applied impartially. Our performance was also evaluated by the number of cases we processed.

These values—efficiency, fairness, responsiveness, and respect—are at the heart of our democratic political culture, but it falls to bureaucrats to find sensible compromises between them and to make sure that none systematically overshadow the rest. In this balancing act, bureaucracies perform a crucial public service. This is a service, moreover, that is independent from the policy goals they are instructed to pursue by the government of the day. Bureaucracy functions not merely as an instrument in the pursuit of specified policy goals, but as a crucible in which our abstract values are given practical meaning and the tensions between them worked out. It is in this sense that we can speak of bureaucracy *as* a public good, not just as an instrument *for* the public good.

IT IS WORTH LOOKING at the bureaucratic demands of efficiency, fairness, responsiveness, and respect in greater detail.

The standard of *efficiency* embodies the ideal of good management. Public administrators are entrusted with a limited amount of public resources, and we, as citizens, expect them to make these resources go as far as possible. This means being economical and speedy in the provision of services, and dispensing them to the greatest possible effect.

We can measure the importance of efficiency, as a standard of evaluation, by the stridency of the criticisms that public administration draws when it fails to live up to it. If public service agencies are perpetually threated with budget cuts and staff reductions it is, in part, because they are widely perceived as slow, wasteful, and ineffective.

On its own, however, the standard of efficiency does not capture what is distinctive about public service agencies. Unlike charities or commercial enterprises, such agencies interact with individuals in their capacity as citizens. They do not merely provide services; they provide services that people are entitled to *as a matter of right*.

Moreover, in a democracy, citizens are political equals who have a claim to being treated by their state with equal concern and respect. Public administrators, then, have a duty of *fairness* and impartiality. Here again, the importance of the criterion can be measured by how seriously we take its violation—when officials are accused, for instance, of favoritism, bias, or discrimination.

The third normative standard—of *responsiveness*—captures the thought that no two cases or situations that bureaucrats encounter are exactly alike. If public administration is to be legitimate, it is not enough for it to be impartial and to treat people equally; it must also be attentive to the specificities of their needs, demands, and circumstances. Pierre Rosanvallon has argued that the importance accorded to responsiveness to particularity is a relatively recent transformation within democracy. Democratic citizens, he claims, are no longer willing to accept a one-size-fits-all model of treatment. They expect officials to listen to them and to respond with some flexibility to the specificities of their case. This comes out in a range of familiar criticisms leveled at public service agencies: that they are distant, unconcerned, and immured in red tape.

The requirement of *respect*, finally, overlaps partially with the previous two without being fully covered by them. To be treated with respect is to be treated according to fair standards and with proper attention to the specificity of one's case. But as Jonathan Wolff has argued, it is also to be treated in a way that is neither insulting, demeaning, nor infantilizing. Bureaucracies can be insulting when they lack common courtesy toward clients or when they are unduly suspicious of them.

They can be demeaning when they require recipients to publicly reveal things about themselves they consider shameful as a condition for getting assistance. They can be infantilizing when they treat clients as if they were not capable of making decisions for themselves.

These four normative demands—efficiency, fairness, responsiveness, and respect—capture value commitments that are central to our democratic political culture. They involve a concern, respectively, for the aggregate well-being of citizens, for their equality, for their individual rights, as well as for their autonomy and dignity. These commitments are irreducibly plural. We may prefer to have them in different mixes, but most of us would agree that all of them should be attended to.

The problem, of course, is that these commitments often point in competing directions. The demands of fairness and responsiveness can clash, especially when resources are scarce. Should bureaucrats exhaust all the options available to a particular client or adopt a standard of treatment they could realistically replicate for all? Efficiency is often measured by the number of cases processed. But what if racking up numbers can be achieved by prioritizing easy cases and dispensing with complicated ones? And what about the many facets of respect? The most expedient way to process clients, after all, is to be curt with them.

This is where the moral, as opposed to the merely technical, challenge of implementation begins. How should we weigh these plural demands and strike sensible compromises between them?

These questions are difficult, in part, because a proper answer to them is highly dependent on context and situation. We can develop broad guidelines for how to handle tradeoffs that recur frequently, but there is a limit to how much we can decide cases ex ante without blindly prejudging them. This is why administrative rules and procedures must often coexist with a substantial amount of discretion, and why this discretion must trickle all the way down to the frontlines of public service provision.

TO SAY THAT BUREAUCRATS must attend to a plurality of values is not to say that they are always successful in doing so. Any organization would be hard pressed to be efficient, fair, responsive, and respectful at once—let alone one that is chronically understaffed, underfunded, and forced to operate in a hostile political environment.

Bureaucrats often have no choice but to make difficult tradeoffs between different dimensions of value. In such conditions, it is proper to feel conflicted. It would be worrying, in fact, if one did not.

But while moral conflicts of this kind occur occasionally in our ordinary moral life, three features of frontline work in public service make them particularly hard to bear. The first is that bureaucrats experience these value conflicts relentlessly, since the demand for public services never abates. The second is that any half-measures or compromises can have serious consequences for clients. By accelerating the pace of work, for example, a caseworker might not build an intimate enough rapport for a client to open up about sensitive topics such as domestic violence. Conversely, by slowing it down, other clients might be late on receiving a check they desperately need.

Navigating such conflicts is distressing for bureaucrats because, as a frontline worker, you are personally implicated in the process. As I learned from taking over DeShawn's role as a receptionist, it is not the "bureaucratic state" that lets a client down, but *you*. As a street-level bureaucrat, you are the face of the institution—the immediate cause of clients' despair, frustration, and anger, and the first to witness it.

It is hard not to feel complicit and not to blame yourself. You start wondering whether *you* might in fact be the one failing clients. However hard and conscientiously you work, you cannot shake off the thought that you might have been able to do more or better. How long can you think of yourself as a competent and dedicated public servant when you are forced to flout that ideal daily? Knowing that the problem is structural in nature is little consolation when you are the one who has to make the tough calls, and when you are seen as such by those who bear the consequences of your choices.

Over time the psychological pressure builds and, if left unchecked, takes its toll. Some are able to put up with it by compartmentalizing and distancing themselves from their actions. Others burn out. A great many, however, respond as social psychologists would have us expect: through cognitive distortions that simplify the moral landscape and thereby reduce the sense of conflict they experience. Since they cannot live up to the demands of the role, they narrow their understanding of these demands so as to be able to live up to them.

Frontline bureaucrats often pick one dimension of the role and dedicate themselves unreservedly to it, to the exclusion of others. Some come to think of themselves as caregivers, devoting themselves to particular clients regardless of the consequences. Others become fixated on upholding program requirements and making sure that no one takes unfair advantage of existing provisions. And others become absorbed in seeing clients as rapidly as possible to maximize the number of those they can assist. Moral specialization along these lines emerges as a coping response to the pressures of everyday work. It reduces the sense of conflict that one experiences, at the cost of a reductive understanding of one's responsibilities.

Public service agencies thus find themselves in a bind. The proper implementation of public policy depends on their capacity to foster a workforce attuned to a plurality of values. And yet, the nature of everyday work at the frontlines of public service rewards narrow specialization.

THERE ARE STEPS that bureaucracies and bureaucrats can take to better cope with such a predicament.

At the individual level, the bureaucrats who succeed in retaining a balanced approach to the role are those who learn to live with conflict. They come to accept it as an unavoidable part of the job—one that must be managed, controlled, and toned down to a level that is sustainable. They do so, in part, by deploying a range of everyday practices of the self that allow them to mitigate the psychological strain and preempt the cognitive distortions it would otherwise produce.

Management makes a difference, too. Supervisors can counteract the drift toward reductive dispositions by fostering diverse working groups in which peers with different sensibilities keep one another in check. They can design and calibrate a multidimensional system of incentives to remind workers of the relevant considerations.

Getting that balance right is more an art than a science, but the underlying idea is simple: if we want bureaucracy to attend to a plurality of values, such pluralism must itself be reflected *within* the organization. This is an approach to management that is sensible when we cannot specify in advance what we want bureaucrats to do, but when we know what considerations we want them to be mindful of as they figure it out for themselves.

This stance involves some measure of humility. We want bureaucrats to be respectful and responsive, while recognizing that we cannot spell out precisely what this will entail in a particular context or situation. We also need them to be fair and efficient, while admitting that we cannot elucidate how conflicts between these various desiderata should be handled.

The key to this approach is not just to rely on bureaucrats' judgment, but to make sure they evolve in a decision-making environment that exposes them to the right cues and influences. This approach ("delegate and inform") is a departure from both the rule-saturated model of governance that we typically associate with bureaucracy ("command and control") and from the managerial model that has gradually been replacing it.

Since the 1980s, under the influence of a body of ideas known variously as Reinventing Government or New Public Management, public service agencies have incorporated a vast array of managerial practices drawn from the private sector. Most prominent among these is performance-based evaluation—the idea that the success of bureaucracy should be assessed primarily by the efficiency with which it delivers on its objectives ("set targets and track").

Focusing on objectives rather than procedures was meant to liberate bureaucrats from the tangle of red tape, boosting their efficiency while providing the public with a more objective standard for accountability. Both aspirations are of course laudable, provided we do not fetishize them. While greater accountability is welcome, setting clear metrics as goals risks displacing or distorting an agency's overall mission. In such cases, we achieve a pyrrhic victory: securing greater control over the actions of bureaucrats at the cost of impoverishing their mandate.

Lest we succumb to such facile temptations, the directives we provide bureaucrats must remain underdetermined. We cannot content ourselves with assessing performance in terms of efficiency or compliance to standards. Bureaucrats, after all, do not merely execute. They must also grapple independently with complex normative questions. To govern them as if they were mere instruments is the surest way to hollow out their moral promise. If bureaucracy is to stand a chance of being a public good, we must evaluate and manage bureaucrats with that in mind.

Free College for All

Marshall Steinbaum

THE MOVEMENT FOR FREE COLLEGE has gained considerable momentum in the past year, in no small part thanks to the sad state in which many college graduates currently find themselves. For decades, we have told young cohorts entering the labor market that if they only get the right skills, they will find steady, rewarding, and remunerative work. But we have not been able to keep that promise, in large part because our understanding of the labor market's dysfunction is built on a theory of human capital that has very little to do with reality. We are now living with the consequences: today's students pay more for degrees in the hope of landing a job for which they are overqualified because the alternative is worse: no job at all.

Meanwhile, as tuition continues to rise, accumulated student debt increasingly constitutes its own economic burden, above and beyond a labor market offering stagnant wages and insufficient, precarious work. Student debt is especially onerous for racial minorities, as the current system relegates those with the least family and community resources to the worst higher education institutions, exacerbating inequality. Couple this with continuing cuts to public higher education and, as David Leonhardt recently put it in the *New York Times*, "It's as if our society were deliberately trying to restrict opportunities and worsen income inequality."

The United States has never had free, high-quality college education. But that does not mean we can't. In the past, we have included world-class public education in our understanding of public goods, and we have successfully expanded public education on the premise that society as a whole benefits from a well-educated population. Previous generations and social movements fought hard to create good educational institutions at public expense. The current generation is discovering why that matters.

BETWEEN 1910 AND 1940, the share of eighteen-year-olds with a secondary education increased from 10 to over 50 percent. In their book *The Race Between Education and Technology* (2007), economists Claudia Goldin and Lawrence Katz credit America's economic advances in the twentieth century to this uniquely American "high school movement." As they describe it: "The public high school was recreated in the early 1900s to be a quintessentially American institution: open, forgiving, gender neutral, practical but academic, universal, and often egalitarian. It was reinvented in a manner that moved it away from its nineteenth-century elitist European origins."

Goldin and Katz also emphasize that the "high school movement" was, on the whole, locally funded and directed. There was no national movement toward universal secondary education, or even systematic federal funding available to states to create their own programs. The only impetus for the high school movement at the national level came from federal land grants to states, which set up agricultural colleges for the higher education of farmers and the professional class. Many states guaranteed undergraduate admission to these institutions to anyone with a high school diploma, which spurred many local school districts to expand their provision of public education from primary to secondary school.

For the most part, though, the high school movement happened because local school districts—hundreds of thousands of them—taxed themselves to build and staff free public high schools.

By 1960 California was attempting a similar educational revolution in the realm of higher education. As the rising baby boom generation seemed poised to demand more higher education than any of its predecessors, the state wanted to make high-quality college more accessible. The resulting Master Plan for Higher Education, devised by the University of California's president, Clark Kerr, vastly expanded the University of California system and created the California State system from the state's teachers colleges. It also expanded access to community colleges for remedial education and to aid the transition to traditional higher education. The Master Plan set out to make educational advancement solely a matter of individual proficiency, not family background or ability to pay. The result paralleled what Goldin and Katz observe about the high school movement: that it was open, forgiving, practical but academic, and, above all, egalitarian.

But while California's model was widely lauded and enacted in other states and cities, albeit with a less unified and ambitious vision, the federal government chose a different route with the Higher Education Act of 1965—a decision with reasons and repercussions that form a major part of the background for today's student debt crisis. Instead of funding institutions, the federal government funded students. Why?

The main reason was race. At the time, the federal government already had its hands full enforcing the Supreme Court's mandate for integrated elementary and secondary education. As the 1960s turned into the 1970s, the political difficulties enforcing that mandate with court-ordered integration plans and busing became ever more severe, making racial integration seem structurally impossible. For many, trying to add higher education to the mix was a bridge too far.

Moreover, while one of the ultimate goals of the civil rights movement was to integrate the grand public edifices created by the Progressive and New Deal eras, the potent backlash to that goal ended up eroding those same public goods for everyone. Once it became politically and rhetorically impossible to note the existence of racial exclusion in the public sphere, a new ideology of economic individualism came to dominate federal and state policymaking. This included geographic relocation—suburbanization—as a method of avoiding integrated schools and neighborhoods, evading the reach of the federal judiciary and a cautious Congress. Indeed, subsidized mortgage lending in all-white neighborhoods ensured that even as one political movement integrated the economy and society, another resegregated it.

In this respect, Title IV of the Higher Education Act of 1965 led the way; it was individualistic from the start. Reflective of the "human capital" ideology and economic theory of the day, the Higher Education Act facilitated individual choice in selecting (and gaining admission to) institutions that operated within an already-stratified system. Rather than funding institutions and telling them to provide education of a certain standard for all comers (subject to entrance requirements)—what economists would call a "pooling equilibrium"—it funded students, who could then be sorted into a "separating equilibrium," effectively stratifying the sector by race and class.

The aforementioned theory of "human capital" behind these policies holds that students would choose their level of educational attainment by comparing earnings, net of tuition, and opportunity cost. In this story, the policy failure in higher education comes about if students are unable to secure financing for their education before their career starts, thanks to the impossibility of collateralizing human capital, and the resulting high cost of borrowing with unsecured debt. Therefore students cannot undertake a profitable investment in their future earnings unless their families can support them. The solution to this "market failure" was to supply government-guaranteed student loans, thus ensuring access to higher education that will pay off ex post, both for borrowers and for the lender.

The thinking at the time maintained that if students had access to loans, they had access to education, thus negating the need to create the grand edifices in the public sector that characterized earlier eras and led to the civil rights conflicts over universal access. The "quintessentially American" model of education had changed from free and equal high-quality public education to private or privatized institutions and student debt. While government-guaranteed student loans solved a narrow policy problem—an incomplete capital market for financing higher education—they carried the implication that there was no other problem to be solved.

THIS CONCEPTION OF HIGHER EDUCATION thrived for the next several decades, as student populations became larger, more diverse by race and gender, and, simultaneously, more indebted. However, things started to go seriously wrong in the mid-2000s, as state budget crises following the 2000–1 recession led to the decline of state funding for higher education and the concurrent rise of the for-profit higher education sector.

Previously serving only a few technical niches with narrow credentialing mechanisms, for-profit chains such as the University of Phoenix found a massively expanded market by offering flexible, non-traditional degree options suited to older students, as well as a wider variety of degree offerings for those seeking service sector employment. The deregulation of accreditation standards in the mid-2000s also helped aid the boom, since for-profit schools were suddenly eligible for federally guaranteed student loans.

This vast expansion of the federal student loan program can be interpreted as the most ambitious federal labor market policy of the past several decades. Although it did not really start in terms of sheer numbers until the 2000s, its roots can be found in part in economic scholarship and popular discussion of the economy from the 1990s. The story told at the time was as follows: sectoral transformation in the economy increased the need for workers with high human capital, which corresponded with high educational attainment in the form of a college degree. According to this interpretation, the reason why wage inequality rose in the 1980s and '90s was that rising demand for skilled workers confronted a relative slow increase in the supply of skilled workers—hence higher wages for the skilled and rising inequality overall. This theory was even tweaked and extended to explain overall macroeconomic growth dynamics through the lens of aggregate human capital.

This human capital–oriented approach to the labor market gradually morphed into a normative claim: to increase wages and economic growth, we should increase human capital by expanding higher education. The federal student loan program, in conjunction with increased enrollment, became the policy mechanism for accomplishing this. The normative implication was even extended to individual workers: if you want higher wages, increase your educational attainment and take on debt to do so. The debt would "pay for itself" with the increased earnings available to those with more education. But this theory was premised on the idea that the value of higher education credentials remains constant or increases, even as more people obtain them, because wages are set by worker productivity and productivity is increased by more education. That assumption proved false.

Formal and informal credentialization played a key role in driving would-be workers to acquire more debt-funded education, at all levels.

For example, the reforms enacted by the Personal Responsibility and Work Opportunity Reconciliation Act of 1996 required welfare recipients to either have a job or be in "re-training." This drove recipients to seek out certificates from overpriced, predatory institutions, as Tressie McMillan Cottom notes in her book *Lower Ed* (2017).

States also enacted laws requiring teachers to obtain master's degrees in their field of instruction and early education professionals to have bachelor's degrees, both as part of the "standards" movement in education reform—in many cases, without salary increases commensurate with the debt required. The rising prevalence of state-level "occupational licensing" often meant enacting similar attainment requirements to practice as professionals in an increasing number of fields. These formal examples of credentialization through overt policy do not remotely encompass its full impact, which is often achieved informally: when jobs are scarce, employment tends to go to those with the highest educational attainment, leading educational credentials to filter down to lower-paying jobs.

The theory of human capital also provided a convenient pretext for cuts to state higher education budgets. Because college was seen as a good investment in future earnings, state legislatures averse to tax increases saw no problem in shifting education expenditures from their budgets to individual students as demand for higher education rose. And the federal government, its apparatus of subsidized and guaranteed loans now fully developed, was ready to pick up the slack. Since an expansion of human capital was thought to foster economic growth, the long-term, aggregate gain from expanding the stock of outstanding debt and filtering it down the wage distribution to people who would previously have gotten their start in the labor market without higher education (or with less of it) apparently outweighed the risks.

In this sense, federal student debt policy looks a lot like federal home mortgage policy during the inflation of the housing bubble. And as the financial crisis of 2007–8 revealed, there are indeed risks associated with debt-financed assets—they do not continue to increase in value indefinitely. Ironically, though, the end of a dramatic expansion of secured loans in the form of home mortgages was the beginning of the heyday of unsecured loans in the form of student debt. The huge increase in demand for higher education belied the widespread sense, again, that security in the labor market was to be found in credentials that ensured access to the jobs of the future. Since 2000 student debt has clearly followed cycles in the labor market: there are large increases in student debt when enrollment expands during recessions, and a leveling off when the economy partly recovers.

The problem, though, is that each of the last two labor market recoveries has been slow and inadequate compared to those that came before. Consequently once student debt has accumulated, it is increasingly difficult to pay off. The repayment trajectories for successive cohorts of borrowers entering repayment have worsened, to the point that those who theoretically started repayment in 2013 actually have more debt now than when they started, thanks to deferred interest, forbearance, re-enrollment, income-based repayment, and outright delinquency.

These problems are particularly acute for minority borrowers, who are more likely to end up in for-profit, high-tuition institutions that offer poor job prospects; who face discrimination in the labor and credit markets; and who have less family wealth to draw on either in financing higher education upfront or in cushioning the burden of student debt. Holding other demographic variables constant, minority students take on more debt and use it to buy more education than their white counterparts, suggesting that "extra" education—and its accompanying debt—is a prerequisite for minorities to beat the competition for scarce jobs in a discriminatory labor market.

FREE COLLEGE OFFERS A SOLUTION to this sad state of affairs. So long as it was regulated in a way that ensures options for non-traditional students, free higher education would all but end the predatory for-profit sector. In addition, by acting as a "public option," free higher education would serve as a check on the market as a whole. Similar to electric utilities (or banking, health care, and now Internet access), public options offer a compelling vision for disciplining the market to serve, rather than exploit, its participants. Finally, free higher education would also level the racial playing field, mitigating the disparities that arise from inequality in parental and household wealth.

It may seem counterintuitive to suggest that free college would address the problem of runaway credentialization within the labor market. Wouldn't making higher education free also make it more abundant—and hence even less valuable than it already is? This interpretation, however, fails to understand the actual role higher education is currently playing in the labor market: as a tollbooth to decent jobs. That tollbooth is currently expensive and discriminatory, whereas free college would be much cheaper and reduce racial inequalities in access to high-quality institutions.

But by itself, free college will not solve racial inequality in higher education. The public higher education sector is already highly segregated, with minority-serving institutions having borne a disproportionate share of recent state austerity. In too many cases, flagship universities offer de facto preferential admission to white and out-of-state students, especially after recent Supreme Court rulings curtailed their ability to mitigate these inequalities through explicit race-based admissions policies.

What we need, then, is a *Brown v. Board of Education* for higher education: a federal policy of desegregation that would ensure not just that some option in the public system exists regardless of race, but that access to the entire system is available regardless of race, and that the system as a whole is less stratified. This would necessarily reduce inequality within American higher education. In this era of credentialization, when higher education is an absolute prerequisite to getting a job that pays better than minimum wage, we cannot stop until the sector is recast not as a way of preserving and amplifying cross-generational inequality, but of mitigating it.

The heartening news is that we have done this before. While the high school movement really was a magnificent achievement, many southern states lagged behind the rest of the country in providing public secondary education because of racism. The whole concept of public goods was threatening to the South, a region of the country that used discrimination to uphold racial hierarchy at all levels of government and throughout its economy. And yet, the high school movement did eventually expand in the South—most significantly due to the federally led desegregation of southern public education following *Brown v. Board of Education* (1954) and the long battle waged throughout the 1950s and '60s to have the decision enforced in deeply hostile territory.

That battle was won through the logic of public goods. Once that logic was abandoned for an individualistic interpretation of education, those grand edifices were hollowed out, as those able to secure what they wanted with private means decamped for the suburbs and for private schools and universities. From this vantage point, they were happy to see the old system crumble.

As we look back to the first half of the twentieth century to rediscover the logic of public goods, it is crucial to remember two things: public goods do not survive when we let the privileged opt out, and if we make them racially inclusive, the pressure for opt-outs intensifies. Given these antagonistic truths, we cannot pretend public options automatically sustain themselves politically. Success will require an unfailing commitment to universal access, even to the point of prohibiting the privileged from taking their business elsewhere.

Steinbaum

A Public Good Gone Bad

Tracey Meares

THE WALLS OF THE STAIRCASE of Yale Law School, where I teach, are covered with plain white sheets of paper emblazoned with names in black ink. Rekia Boyd. Michael Brown. Sandra Bland. Eric Garner. These names have lived on these walls since a group of students initiated a Say Their Names project in 2015. The group's goal was to encourage those of us working and studying at Yale to engage daily with an issue that fundamentally implicates justice.

However, the best way to solve the epidemic of police violence against black Americans is far from obvious, and it should not be surprising that the solutions advanced by communities of color often run counter to conventional solutions. In some communities marked by extreme levels of violent crime—those one would think most in need of police—residents are calling for a complete and total end to policing. Mychal Denzel Smith, author of *Invisible Man, Got the Whole*

World Watching (2016), captured this sentiment in a piece he wrote for the *Nation*:

> In 1966, James Baldwin wrote . . . , "the police are simply the hired enemies of this population. They are present to keep the Negro in his place and to protect white business interests, and they have no other function." This remains as true today as it was in 1966, only now we have bought into the myth of police "serving and protecting" wholesale. What do you do with an institution whose core function is the control and elimination of black people specifically, and people of color and the poor more broadly? You abolish it.

Abolish the police? Unthinkable? Consider Chicago, where the homicide rate is among the ten most deadly in the United States, and the nonfatal shooting problem is even worse. Yet residents of Chicago's most challenged neighborhoods still find it difficult to swallow the notion that they must endure proactive policing tactics in order to be "safe." Many grassroots initiatives in the city have sought to prove that alternative methods of crime reduction can be more effective than policing. For example, the organization MASK hosts a free community picnic every day on a corner known for its violence.

As the example of MASK highlights, police abolitionists' position and methods are more nuanced and compelling than their critics typically credit them with being. Mariame Kaba has spent decades in Chicago teaching about prison and police abolitionism, drawing on arguments advanced by Angela Davis in the 1990s. Kaba understands that it would be unrealistic to simply shift the burden of police abolition to victims of violent crime by asking them to not call the police, which is often how the movement is caricatured. Her abolition project is more complex: "For me prison abolition is two things: It's the complete and utter dismantling of prison and policing and surveillance as they currently exist within our culture. And it's also the building up of new ways of intersecting and new ways of relating with each other."

I agree with Kaba: policing as we know it must be abolished before it can be transformed. One path to that goal is to recenter policing's fundamental nature as a public good.

Aspects of public infrastructure such as highways, street lighting, and clean water are public goods. In technical terms this means goods that are nonrivalrous and nonexcludable: anyone can enjoy them without diminishing their supply, and no one in the relevant group (e.g., a given city or nation) can be excluded even if they cannot afford to pay. The state typically funds public goods through taxes because the state has a vested interest in making these goods available to its citizens and cannot rely on the market to provide them as they are not necessarily—or even ideally—profitable. National defense is a classic public good, and local policing similarly falls under the conceptual category. Unsurprisingly, most of us would think it extremely unwise—silly, even—to refuse national security or policing, just as it would seem ridiculous to forego street lights, clean water, or sidewalks.

Yet the advocacy of police abolitionists helps us see the limits of framing policing as a public good. How should we think about our public goods when they go bad? In the same way that the residents of Flint, Michigan, have a right to express outrage about the water they were provided, can't we rightly object when the policing provided to us by the state fails our communities?

For example, New York's former mayor Michael Bloomberg and former police commissioner Raymond Kelly argued that the city's massive stop-and-frisk program—in which police stopped hundreds of thousands of residents, many unconstitutionally—largely benefitted the very people who complained about it. Bloomberg and Kelly claimed that the program kept violent crime at historic lows. But many of the individuals subjected to these searches—a significant number of whom were stopped multiple times a year—disagreed with this assessment. Their dissatisfaction gives credence to Elinor Ostrom's prescient 1973 analysis that providing a policing service to some usually means doing a disservice to others. To make sense of the police abolitionists' call, we must first appreciate that how we feel about *whether* policing exists is intimately tied up with *what kind* of policing people believe the state is capable of producing, given their life experiences.

Those who dismiss abolitionists' call for an end to policing assume that policing necessarily prefigures public safety. To them it is nonsensical for residents of high-crime neighborhoods to say that they want less policing, as this is tantamount to saying that they wish violence would befall them. One problem is that the critics of police abolition define public safety very narrowly. Their primary concern is the police's role in keeping us safe from each other, but they ignore the fact that security from government overreach and oppression is also a key element of public safety. Majoritarians such as Bloomberg and Kelly value freedom from private predation over security from state violence, an unsurprising position given that their social status insulates them from the state's most intrusive manifestations, those endured daily by people of color and the poor.

When the public at large experiences the "good" of policing only by concentrating the costs of producing that good on a small group—such as black people, and particularly black men—it is hard to say that the good is "good" or even truly public. We need to create a kind of policing that we *all* can enjoy.

POLICE TRANSFORMATION REQUIRES deep thinking about what it means to say that a public good is both public and good. When one considers the racialized origins of policing in America—from its roots in nineteenth-century slave patrols to its build-up during the early twentieth century as an immigrant-control brigade—it is clear that a necessary first step to redeeming this public good is to find a new symbolic language for thinking about its role in society. This is particularly crucial with regard to the role that police play in generating our understanding of ourselves as citizens—noting that, in both historical examples above, police served to enforce strict limits on who could enjoy the rights of citizenship. Police officers are state authorities who play a critical role in helping people to decipher their environment and where they fit in society. Criminologist Ian Loader and sociologist Aogán Mulcahy put it this way:

> [Police are] an interpretive lens through which people make sense of, and give order to, their world . . . a vehicle that enables individuals and groups to make sense of their past, form judgements on the present, and project various imagined futures. As an institution intimately concerned with the viability of the state . . . policing remains closely tied to the maintenance of ontological security, the production of subjectivities, and the articulation of collective identities.

British Commonwealth scholars have led the way in demonstrating this phenomenon empirically. By focusing on policing in Australia, for example, criminologists Ben Bradford, Kristina Murphy, and Jonathan Jackson examined how people's views are modified by encounters with police. They found that fair treatment by police increases a person's identification with national identity, while poor treatment undermines it. Bradford, Murphy, and Jackson conclude that police can be integral to how people think of themselves as citizens. In a related study, Bradford conducted extensive interviews with young men of color in London, determining that interactions with police were especially important for men whose color and immigration status make them feel already unsure of their position in society.

Scholars of procedural justice note that people generally care much more about how they are treated by police than whether those police are effective crime fighters or make decisions that benefit them personally. People of all races and genders wish to be treated with dignity, respect, and concern for their rights; that this minimal expectation sets such a surprisingly high bar means that it offers a compelling starting point for thinking about police reform across conventional social barriers.

So, what can we do? In 2015 I had the honor of serving on President Obama's Task Force on 21st Century Policing, along with a diverse group of ten other Americans drawn from police leadership, law, social justice initiatives, and NGOs. We created a document detailing fifty-nine recommendations to build trust and legitimacy in policing while continuing to advance public safety. Many of those recommendations focused on better training of police, attention to community policing, caring for the most vulnerable, focusing on officer safety and wellness, and ensuring accountability and oversight of police. In some ways the recommendations seem workaday or even anodyne. But in reality even the most basic among them—such as a recommendation that agencies be honest about their past, acknowledging "the role of policing in past and present injustice and discrimination and how it is a hurdle to the promotion of community trust"—has proven to be incredibly difficult for many if not most agencies. Further steps, such as holding officers criminally accountable for killing unarmed civilians, seem almost impossible.

Policing must reorient itself around a new set of goals; we *must* abandon the project of "proactive policing." Too many officers and agencies proceed with their work as if the pursuit of crime reduction is self-justifying. Public safety, narrowly defined as crime reduction, simply does not provide a warrant for overly aggressive proactive policing approaches. Attention to co-production of public security with communities should be policing's primary goal. Many, including many police officers, will think this recommendation radical. After all, the historically low crime levels that we enjoy today correlate at least in part with the innovation of holding policing agencies accountable for crime levels, rather than only their response times to victims' calls. But the fact that public trust has not increased even while crime has plummeted over the last thirty years is a key indication that we took a wrong turn.

Strict adherence to constitutional law by police is both necessary and alone inadequate to solve the crisis we face. The Obama Justice Department's Civil Rights Division initiated more pattern-or-practice consent decrees than any prior administration. These settlements sought to spur police reform by allowing departments to commit to reforming discriminatory patterns without having to admit wrongdoing. Such efforts are designed to bring police departments into compliance with constitutional guarantees, but constitutional compliance does not necessarily lead to public trust. Police lawfulness does not seem to be tightly connected to how people *perceive* the fairness of police actions, and therefore does not likely correlate to how much the public *trusts* police. The average citizen does not conflate lawfulness with rightfulness; in short, the public does not evaluate police actions through the same highly technical and morally neutral lens of legality that police and other legal authorities use. Instead people reference the procedural justice factors reviewed earlier to come to conclusions about whether police acted fairly. Obviously, police must bring their activities in line with constitutional minimums, but we must also demand that agencies pay attention to *how* they engage with citizens. Agencies must create policy *with* neighborhood residents, not for them. Agencies must be transparent and consistent. Police officers must act as agents for the principals they serve.

Taking the agency–community relationship seriously implies a host of changes that are about more than having police meet the legal minimums. Some of this work can be done through legislation, but much of it will require new accountability accords between the police and the public. Los Angeles' Board of Police Commissioners and Seattle's Community Police Commission provide intriguing examples. In both cases civilians lead the way in setting policy goals and direction for the city's policing agencies, rather than the other way around.

Probably the most important change we can make is to require policing agencies to take preservation of life seriously. Everyone's life. A commitment to preserving life, in concert with no longer treating crime reduction as the highest goal, will necessarily rewrite the aims of policing. Officers currently treat traffic stops as necessary and perilous operations. If police work together with the communities they serve, it might become clear that stopping someone for a minor traffic violation is not even something police should be doing.

Disadvantaged communities ought not give up policing any more than they should give up public schools, electricity, or water. But likewise they must not trade security for majoritarian conceptions of public safety. If police cannot find a way to change in ways that will better serve the people, then, yes, their footprint should be reduced. But I still think we can do better than that impoverished second best.

The Worth of Water

Meghan O'Gieblyn

A FRIEND WHO GREW UP, as I did, near Lake Michigan once remarked that the Great Lakes were prone, more than any other natural feature, to "plagues of a biblical scale." I knew what he meant: to live on those waters was to bear witness to a series of ecological dramas, each one as spectacular as it was sudden. One summer toxic algae blooms dyed the channels a bioluminescent green and everyone who swam in them developed mouth blisters. A few years later, the perch died and washed up on the beach in such multitudes you could smell them from the other side of the dunes. After particularly cold winters, the tides rose high and portions of the beach disappeared entirely. Other times the water would recede far beyond the sandbars, leaving behind a vast stretch of pocked and rocky mudflats—land that looked stricken, or cursed.

Plagues are always meant as warnings. But unlike my friend, I had never considered these events in moralistic terms; it was not clear to me that we were being punished, or even implicated. The fluctuations were unpredictable, after all, and rarely repeated, and the lake bore none of the familiar signs of dystopian ecology that I had come to associate with narratives about climate change—no beaches smeared with oil, no waters clouded with chemical waste. In fact, throughout my adolescence, Lake Michigan was visibly cleaner than it had been in decades—so clear, on some mornings, that its water could, if bottled, pass for vodka. If anything, these signs seemed to belong to a more ancient cosmology, one driven not by divine law and its transgression but by the whims of some fractious pantheon whose moods were mercurial and sublimated into natural events. Their meaning was anyone's guess.

Climate models warn that the coming apocalypse will be one of water. Glaciers will calve in thundering cascades, the rising oceans will erode the coasts, and droughts will make whole countries uninhabitable. Yet, more often than not, the most immediate threats to our resources bear little resemblance to these lurid forecasts. The present dangers express themselves, increasingly, in ways that are insidious and irregular, and when they do manage to catch our attention, it is easy to dismiss them as flukes.

There was a time not so long ago when the disruptions to our waters were more predictable. This is particularly true of the Great Lakes, the abode of more than 20 percent of the planet's surface freshwater, and the subject of Dan Egan's important new book, *The Death and Life of the Great Lakes* (2017). Around the middle of the last century, Egan notes, these bodies of water were in dire straits, and the signs of trouble were obvious to anyone with eyes and a nose. Large portions of the five lakes were clouded with industrial waste, and hundreds of square miles of waters were declared "dead." Cleveland's Cuyahoga River, which flows into Lake Erie, served as the dumping ground for the steel industry's runoff, and was for some time so slicked with oil that it would spontaneously burst into flames.

This damage was the inevitable outcome of two centuries of careless pillaging by generations of Americans who regarded nature as the raw material of empire, a wilderness to be conquered and subdued. It is an outlook evident in Alexis de Tocqueville's remarks upon arriving in 1831 on the virgin shores of Lake Huron: "Nothing is missing but civilized man, and he is at the door." To some extent, the history of this region reads like a cautionary tale about the perils of hubris. The nineteenth and early twentieth centuries were characterized by grandiose engineering projects—the Erie Canal, the Saint Lawrence Seaway, and the Chicago Sanitary and Ship Canal—that were designed to connect the Great Lakes to other bodies of water, carving new paths for commercial freighters. At the time, these projects were roundly heralded as triumphs. Walter Cronkite declared the opening of the Saint Lawrence Seaway in 1959 as the "greatest engineering feat of our time," one that is "reshaping a continent, completing the job nature had begun thousands of years ago." In the end, these manmade channels opened the doors to a host of invasive species that destroyed the lakes' native fish populations and led to several major die-offs.

The past half-century has been spent atoning for these blunders. The Clean Water Act of 1972 imposed a system of regulations that dramatically improved the quality of the nation's waterways. As a result the number of American lakes and rivers listed as unsafe for swimming and fishing has since been cut in half. Some of the destroyed natural barriers to the Great Lakes have been replaced with manmade ones, stanching the progress of more invasive fish. These remedies were generated, in part, by a shift in public opinion about the role of human activity in the natural world—a change so dramatic that today the older rhetoric of conquering and reshaping nature reads as bewilderingly naïve. We have, if nothing else, a greater sense of humility, a chastened sense of our place in the order of things.

Which is not to say we have made our peace with these waters. Over the past few decades, Egan argues, humans have done equal, if not worse, damage to the lakes through negligence, lethargy—and occasionally even through good intentions. A seemingly minor loophole in the Clean Water Act, for instance, allowed freighters coming in from the Atlantic to dump their ballast water in the Great Lakes. That water contained zebra and quagga mussels, species native to the Black and Caspian Seas that have no natural predators in the Great Lakes. The mussels have now proliferated to the point that they completely blanket the bottom of Lake Michigan, shore to shore. They have decimated native fish populations, caused several botulism outbreaks, and slowly made their way down the channels to the Mississippi River drainage basin, which covers 40 percent of the continental United States. Thanks to all those manmade channels and seaways, the fate of the Great Lakes is now intricately enlaced with the rest of our nation's waters. Lake Mead's canyon walls are blackened with mussels, and the invaders have gummed up the cooling system of the Hoover Dam, which generates electricity for more than 1.5 million people. In these western states alone, the infestation has cost hundreds of millions of dollars; the Great Lakes states have spent billions.

Another threat that conservation acts have struggled to address is agricultural runoff, which is considered a "nonpoint source" pollutant, an ill that seeps from diffuse and diverse sources rather than a discrete point of origin. Farm fertilizers are chock full of phosphorus, and trickle into the lakes in alarming quantities, especially because farmers in the region have increasingly turned to no-till techniques. These practices are undeniably good for the soil—the farmers have adopted them at the urging of environmental groups worried about erosion—but they make it easier for runoff to spill into the local waters before it is absorbed by the crops. The runoff is selectively filtered by the invasive mussels, whose presence in the lakes has served to stimulate the growth of algae blooms, which in turn release toxins and have sucked the oxygen out of large stretches of water.

Of course an algae bloom, or a ship prow clinging with mussels, has none of the dystopian drama of a flaming river. The omens of disaster are more subtle today than they were in the past, and Egan worries that these signs will fail to ignite the kind of widespread public outrage that led to reforms such as the Clean Water Act. Even the gorgeously limpid waters of Lake Michigan should, technically, be read as a sign of trouble. The reason the Great Lakes are so clear is that these invasive mussels have devastated the native ecology. "This is not the sign of a healthy lake," Egan writes; "it's the sign of a lake having the life sucked out of it."

In the end, Egan's book serves as a reminder that the ecological universe we inhabit is vastly connected and cannot be easily mended by humility and good intentions. If the sin of past generations was hubris, our own vices are those that metastasize in the fine print: the loopholes we tolerate or overlook in conservation acts, the court rulings that refuse to impose a concrete deadline, the jargonish clauses in shipping contracts—and also the blitheness of all of us who continue to enjoy these waters, oblivious to signs of trouble.

GRANTED, THERE ARE DISASTERS that still manage to get our attention. When the story of the Flint water crisis broke in early 2015, it became a fixation of the national media, a baffling instance of government incompetence and resource mismanagement. City and state officials had assured the citizens of Flint that it was safe to drink from city taps even after the faucets began dispensing foul brown muck and health officials had confirmed an outbreak of Legionnaires' disease. They continued to insist that the water was safe long after a GM plant discovered the water was corroding its auto parts, and local pastors were forced to stop performing baptisms. In total more than 9,000 Flint children under the age of 6 were exposed to toxic levels of lead, and the poisoned water made its way into some 18,000 homes. The story dominated national headlines and op-ed articles, where it was all too often used as fodder, on both the right and the left, for existing political debates.

Poison on Tap (2016) is the first book to attempt a detailed and objective retrospective of the crisis, tackling the perplexing web of actions that led to its nadir. Published by *Bridge Magazine*—a publication of the nonprofit think tank Center for Michigan, and one of the few outlets that covered the crisis from the start—the book collects two years' worth of the magazine's reportage on the crisis, alongside leaked government emails and intricately compiled timelines of who knew what when. What emerges from these documents is perhaps the first truly comprehensive, chronological narrative of the catastrophe, one that began in 2013 with Flint's decision to pull out of the Detroit pipeline to Lake Huron, which had been its longtime water source, in order to connect to the new Karegnondi pipeline. It was a decision made primarily for economic reasons, a plan endorsed by the emergency city manager, who had his eye on the books and the bottom line.

From that moment on, the story reads as a kind of morality play, one with a particularly tortured plotline and a stage overcrowded with actors collectively taking on the role of Vice. Among this hapless cast are the Detroit Water and Sewage Department agents who terminated Flint's contract early, out of spite; the city's emergency financial managers who advised switching over to the Flint River as a temporary, cost-effective solution; the water lab team that was unprepared for the switch; the city officials who failed to anticipate the necessity of corrosion control; the state Department of Environmental Quality that discounted early warnings that lead, bacteria, and other contaminants were leaching into the water; the governor who was distracted by a triumphant coast-to-coast reelection tour. Each of these officials initially denied their role in the incident, shifting the responsibility to other agencies, though in the final analysis, it seems that the blame must be parceled out among them all. This was, at any rate, what the activist Erin Brockovich concluded in 2015. "Now is not the time for the blame game," she wrote in a Facebook post that called national attention to the crisis. "Everyone is responsible from the top down: USEPA, Michigan Department of Environmental Quality, the State of Michigan and the local officials."

After finishing *Poison on Tap*, I had no choice but to agree with her. And yet, how tedious it was to weed through so many documents and reports only to encounter no central malevolence, no locus of evil, but rather an immense volume of petty human error—dozens upon dozens of warnings discounted, actions postponed, and dangers overlooked. In early June, it was announced that five public officials, including the director of Michigan's Department of Health and Human Services, were being charged with involuntary manslaughter for ignoring the outbreak of Legionnaires' disease. But this belated delivery of justice could not but seem insufficient, perhaps even arbitrary. The comments sections of the news articles were dominated by citizens asking why similar accountability had not been demanded of the governor, or other officials who were equally responsible. The "blame game" in such cases becomes an endless spiral of culpability. The Flint crisis stands, if nothing else, as a testament to the fact that we live in a highly developed modern bureaucracy, a structure of our own making that is every bit as complex and mystifying as the ecological systems we are still struggling to understand. In both realms, it is increasingly difficult to grasp the scope of our actions and the extent to which our errors are bound up with the lives of others. Beneath the specific blunders of these elected officials lurked a host of larger systemic issues—poverty, deindustrialization—that conspired to make Flint particularly vulnerable to the crisis. These underlying problems are so vast and bewildering that as I read the book, I was at times overcome by a sense of uneasiness that bordered on paranoia. It did not seem impossible that I myself was implicated in the crisis.

This anxiety is, of course, a condition of late modernity, one that has escalated steadily over the course of the last half-century and was memorably dramatized by the TV show *The Wire* (2002–8), which imagined evil as an emergent entity made up of a billion tiny errors and oversights. It is an anxiety that perhaps reached its apex during the Obama years, when there existed on the left a gnawing conviction that all of us were, to some degree, complicit in the murky dealings of global capitalism, the silent murder by drone and our planet's slow demise.

If this anxiety has lessened somewhat over the past year, it is because we do, finally, have a villain. The Trump era has brought to power a cohort of men who refuse to pay lip service to the narratives of ecological harmony, who speak in the antiquated language of conquering and subduing, and who have taken up, once again, the dusty mantle of Empire. In February of this year, Trump threatened to roll back the Clean Water Rule, which protects seasonal streams and wetlands, in the interest of "promoting economic growth," and his proposed EPA cuts would likely decrease funding for grants that help states to monitor public water systems.

These threats to our waters are real. But perhaps the more insidious danger is the simplicity of this new moral battleground, one that is a welcome, if unacknowledged, relief to the liberal conscience. I say this because I have found it a relief myself. It is far more satisfying to point, definitively, at an external foe than it is to contend with the labyrinthine math of bureaucratic mishaps—or to gaze uncertainly inward. In this new political landscape, good and evil are unambiguous entities existing on opposite sides of a clearly drawn line. It is a world in which complex ethical considerations have given way to shouting matches between those who accept reality and those who deny it, and marching in the name of Science—not any particular philosophy or method, but the whole enterprise, from Copernicus to Mengele—earns one a seat on the right side of history. It is a much easier terrain in which to exist, and yet it in no way reflects the complexity of the actual world that we still inhabit, one in which good intentions count for little, and even the best ideas are capable of wreaking unexpected and irrevocable damage.

Both Egan's book and the story of the Flint crisis suggest that the fate of water security depends upon careful attention to detail, vigilant demands of personal accountability and—perhaps most crucially—public awareness about the complexities of resource management. This is particularly necessary at a time when public goods are targets for privatization, and vulnerable communities such as Flint are subject to emergency management laws that elude the safeguards of local government oversight. Cost-cutting, corruption, and cowing to private corporations are not limited to any one political party, and even the most well-meaning administration can wreak havoc when left to run on its own steam, without attentive public engagement. To abandon this vigilance in favor of a more simplistic morality would be an error with no shortage of potential catastrophic outcomes.

Near the end of Egan's book, he quotes one of Benjamin Franklin's more ominous aphorisms: "When the well is dry, we know the worth of water." It is this warning that has stuck with me over the past few weeks, rattling around my mind in idle moments with the persistence of a riddle. Something about its gloominess, its allusion to assets unappreciated and warnings heeded too late, seems to distill a particularly troubling human tendency—or perhaps merely an American one. It is possible that the true cost of our actions will only emerge in hindsight. Perhaps only after the waters have run dry—or completely subsumed us—will the record show in perfect clarity the accretion of misdeeds that contributed to the degradation of our planet. Though we cannot predict how history will regard our errors, I can only assume that this future reckoning, whatever form it takes, will be as unforgiving as the natural world we inhabit and every bit as sweeping and exhaustive as the structures we have built. Everything will be accounted for; no action will be spared.

O'Gieblyn

Draining the Swamp

Julian C. Chambliss

DONALD TRUMP CALLS his Florida estate, Mar-a-Lago, his "winter White House." This proclamation has been met with derision as well as outrage about the security costs and conflict of interest. But the sheer hucksterism that has defined Trump's ownership—buying the once federally owned estate, overcoming local objections by turning it into an exclusive club, and finally using it, in name only, as a public institution—should also interest us. Often casting himself as an aggrieved party fighting entrenched interests in Palm Beach, Trump's battles there offer a funhouse-mirror version of the common man's struggle against elites. Presented in the rarified air of Palm Beach, Trump's Mar-a-Lago travails foreshadowed his current political narrative.

Moreover, Trump's relationship to Mar-a-Lago and his pursuit of victory there at all costs reveal a regressive vision of community, one that resonates deeply with Florida's history. For almost

150 years, wealthy outsiders have fought an anemic state over who gets to enjoy paradise. Aggressive development opened up Florida for millions of ordinary Americans, but in the absence of an effective state, wealthy interests have hollowed out prospects for working people, degraded the environment, and made the consumption of Florida a rich man's game. Mar-a-Lago reflects the legacy of Florida's past. Given the newly established winter White House, this legacy now belongs to all of us.

MAR-A-LAGO IS A LINK to a historical Florida that was ripe with excesses and engaged in a long struggle over who should control land and resources. The state first began to boom in the last decade of the nineteenth century, when concerns about urban congestion prompted millions of Americans to seek out nature for rejuvenation and relaxation. Doctors recommended Florida for recuperation from a range of ailments, and developers saw an opportunity to package paradise. The sparsely populated, debt-ridden, swampy state became, seemingly overnight, a popular destination.

Hamilton Disston, the head of a large Philadelphia manufacturing company, helped initiate this transformation. After visiting Florida on a fishing trip in 1881, he bought 4 million acres from the state and commenced an ambitious project to turn swamp into usable land. "What is claimed to be the largest purchase of land ever made by a single person in the world occurred today," the *New York Times* announced, while noting the competition from anxious "capitalists of New York and Boston." Disston, at least, was well-intentioned: by draining the Everglades, he hoped to turn the area into productive farmland. But while his agrarian vision failed, his efforts attracted other northern industrialists who would take a different approach.

Henry B. Plant, a railroad magnate, and Henry M. Flagler, a partner in Standard Oil, saw tourism as the path forward for Florida. Both together and separately, the men created a system of railroads and luxury hotels throughout the state. The network linked the western coast to the rest of the United States and allowed trade south to Key West and Cuba. Plant focused mostly on Tampa Bay, where in 1891 he constructed the Tampa Bay Hotel, a 511-room Moorish palace, at a cost of around $3 million, while Flagler's chain of luxurious resort hotels would eventually stretch to Key West, embellishing the image of Florida as an idyllic wonderland.

Flagler ended up setting an aesthetic standard that would define the state, one that infused a sybaritic flavor into the built environment. For the construction of the Ponce de Leon Hotel in St. Augustine, he sent architects John Carrere and Thomas Hastings to Spain. For his signature hotels in Palm Beach, notable architects such as Addison Mizner constructed Mediterranean-inspired villas with sun-drenched patios and massive rooms for entertaining. But Flagler's style rested on his reputation for building huge structures in sparsely populated areas—an approach that meant the end for the Styx Community, hundreds of working-class blacks (and whites) who had built Flagler's Palm Beach hotels. By 1910 most of the black workers had been forcibly relocated to West Palm Beach.

Paradise was for sale, but at a cost. Men such as Plant and Flagler propagated and profited from the idea of a modernizing New South, but in reality the region remained primarily agrarian. The end of Reconstruction returned Democrats to power across the region, and these "Redeemers" fought to undo reforms such as voting rights and pursued fiscal policies that undercut public goods such as education. White and African American laborers and small farmers felt the effects most profoundly, leading to a regressive economic order that African American writer T. Thomas Fortune described as a "pauperization" of laboring people across the South.

An alliance of farmers in the South and Midwest tried to fight back. By 1890 National Farmers' Alliance and the Colored Farmers' Alliance were a force in Florida state politics. Candidates for state office sought

Alliance endorsement and those candidates were a majority of those elected to the 1890 state legislature. The national meeting of the Alliance in Ocala, in December 1890, marked the high point of the movement. The policies articulated there became known as the "The Ocala Demands," and included the abolition of national banks, the end of futures speculation, and the reclaiming of excess lands held by railroads. These demands served as the basis of the People's (or Populist) Party Platform in 1891, but despite the radical resistance, the Democratic Party prevailed. By the start of the twentieth century, most of Florida's political leaders had fully embraced big developers as the necessary fuel for Florida's future.

BEFORE LONG, Palm Beach County became ground zero for a particular flavor of development. The barrier island became defined by its luxury and exclusivity, inspiring new communities that sprouted up across the bay in the state's 1920s land boom, including Boca Raton (1925), Coral Gables (1925), and Deerfield Beach (1925). By 1927 Mar-a-Lago became one of the grandest creations in the extravagant tradition that defined Palm Beach.

Commissioned by Marjorie Merriweather Post, heiress to the cereal fortune, and designed by Marion Sims Wyeth, who specialized in catering to clients' fantasies, Mar-a-Lago (which means "between the sea and the lake") brought Spanish, Venetian, and Portuguese architectural elements together in a 110,000-square-foot mansion. The site became a showcase for the architectural remnants and furnishings Post acquired while traveling in Europe. As a social force in Washington, D.C., and Palm Beach—one of her husbands, Joseph E. Davies, was the former ambassador to the Soviet Union—Post's Mar-a-Lago parties did not disappoint. For one she invited Ringling Brothers and Barnum & Bailey Circus to set up on the lawn; for another, she brought down the entire cast of a Broadway show.

Post resided in the home until her death in 1973, at which point she left the estate to the United States. The grandeur of Post's lifestyle seemingly informed this decision; she had entertained elites in her homes, after all, and she willed a suitable location for the nation to do the same. But Mar-a-Lago never fulfilled her vision. Much of the estate was mothballed while under government control, including covering much of the furniture and wall hangings, letting the floors go unpolished, and cutting back to a skeleton maintenance crew. At an estimated cost of a million dollars a year, it was too expensive to keep up. After seven years, the Department of Interior under the Carter administration returned the property to the Post Foundation. But while the estate struggled, Florida was booming.

After World War II, the Florida dream had become an achievable commodity for many. Retirees and a constant flow of new families grew the state's population, transforming vacation towns into cities. The boom delivered steady economic growth, but with the influx of newcomers, sustaining the promise of the Florida dream has proven difficult. An economy dominated by tourism has caused the state to struggle to provide adequate wages and affordable housing while protecting the environment from overdevelopment.

Between 1950 and 2000, for example, coastal counties in Florida added 10 million new residents. Lobbyists and the construction industry have been able to develop the coastline unabated, increasingly building in spaces that are threatened by erosion and that block public access to the beach. Property owners frequently post "Private Property" signs, even though Florida's coastline is public property. The result is that Florida's public coastline is often hidden in the shadow of wealthy high-rises.

By 1980 state and federal laws attempted to address some of these abuses and reign in future development. It is against this backdrop that Trump bought Mar-a-Lago in 1985 for an estimated $10–15 million, and thus began his 30-year struggle against municipal and county governments.

His plans for Mar-a-Lago seemed to clash with authorities at every turn. For example, in 1992, when he wanted to develop private houses on the estate, the Palm Beach town council rejected the plan. But Florida has a history of weakly defending regulation and pandering to the rich, and Trump's combative attitude, money to burn, and deft use of lawsuits has allowed him to get his way every time. He sued the council over the houses, but then dropped the lawsuit when the council approved his plan to convert the estate into a club. In a similar vein, he used lawsuits to maneuver the county into giving him a lease on public land that he used to create the Trump International Golf Club.

Winning the presidency has given Trump the ultimate tool of validation, erasing the clashes over control that have defined his ownership of Mar-a-Lago. The opulence and exclusivity that made it a white elephant to the national government is what attracted Trump in the first place, and his actions since represent a stance more in tune with the robber barons of the nineteenth century than with the modern regulatory state. Now, as news outlets adopt the custom of referring to Mar-a-Lago as the winter White House, Trump has managed to infuse a regressive legacy from the nineteenth century into a symbol of contemporary political life.

While Floridians are still faced with unresolved questions about education, affordable housing, depressed wages, and environmental degradation, Trump's Mar-a-Lago shamelessly restores a statement about wealth and power from a bygone era. But his dream is also not sustainable. As sea levels rise, a federal program to assess flood risk and bolster Florida's coastal storm protections has been cut from Trump's 2018 budget. Scientists predict that Mar-a-Lago will be underwater by the end of the century.

Sally Ball is the author of *Wreck Me* and *Annus Mirabilis*. An associate professor of English at Arizona State University, Ball is also an associate director of Four Way Books.

Julian C. Chambliss is Professor of History at Rollins College. He is coeditor of the forthcoming *Assemble: Essays on the Modern Marvel Cinematic Universe*.

Joshua Cohen is coeditor of *Boston Review*, member of the faculty of Apple University, and Distinguished Senior Fellow in law, philosophy, and political science at University of California, Berkeley.

Michael Hardt is Professor of Literature at Duke University and author, with Antonio Negri, of *Assembly*.

Bonnie Honig is 2016–17 Chesler-Mallow Senior Research Fellow at the Pembroke Center and Nancy Duke Lewis Professor of Modern Culture and Media and Political Science at Brown University. She is author of *Public Things: Democracy in Disrepair*.

Lauren Jacobs is the Director of Capacity Building and Special Projects for the Partnership for Working Families. She has been an organizer for twenty years and previously served as First Vice President for SEIU.

Elaine Kamarck is a Senior Fellow in the Governance Studies program at Brookings Institute, where she is also Director of the Center for Effective Public Management. A lecturer in Public Policy at the Harvard Kennedy School of Government, she is author of *Why Presidents Fail and How They Can Succeed Again*.

Jacob T. Levy is Tomlinson Professor of Political Theory, Professor of Political Science, and associated faculty in the Department of Philosophy at McGill University. He is the author of *Rationalism, Pluralism, and Freedom*.

Shane McCrae is the author of *Mule, Blood,* and *Forgiveness Forgiveness.* He teaches at Oberlin College and in the brief-residency MFA program at Spalding University.

Tracey Meares is the Walton Hale Hamilton Professor of Law at Yale Law School. She has worked extensively with the federal government and served on President Obama's Task Force on 21st Century Policing.

Meghan O'Gieblyn's work has appeared in *n+1,* the *New York Times,* the *Guardian, Oxford American,* the *Point, Guernica,* and *Threepenny Review.* A collection of her essays is forthcoming.

Craig Santos Perez is Assistant Professor of English at the University of Hawaii, Manoa, and author of two collections of poetry, *from unincorporated territory [hacha]* and *from unincorporated territory [saina].*

K. Sabeel Rahman is Assistant Professor of Law at Brooklyn Law School and author of *Democracy Against Domination.*

Marshall Steinbaum is Senior Economist and Fellow at the Roosevelt Institute and coeditor of *After Piketty: The Agenda for Economics and Equality.*

Bernardo Zacka is Assistant Professor of Political Science at MIT and author of *When the State Meets the Street: Public Service and Moral Agency.*